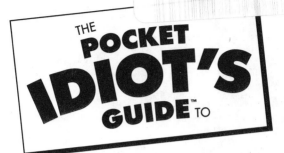

THE
POCKET
IDIOT'S
GUIDE TO

Annuities

by Ken Little

ALPHA

A member of Penguin Group (USA) Inc.

ALPHA BOOKS

Published by the Penguin Group

Penguin Group (USA) Inc., 375 Hudson Street, New York, New York 10014, U.S.A.

Penguin Group (Canada), 10 Alcorn Avenue, Toronto, Ontario, Canada M4V 3B2 (a division of Pearson Penguin Canada Inc.)

Penguin Books Ltd, 80 Strand, London WC2R 0RL, England

Penguin Ireland, 25 St Stephen's Green, Dublin 2, Ireland (a division of Penguin Books Ltd)

Penguin Group (Australia), 250 Camberwell Road, Camberwell, Victoria 3124, Australia (a division of Pearson Australia Group Pty Ltd)

Penguin Books India Pvt Ltd, 11 Community Centre, Panchsheel Park, New Delhi—110 017, India

Penguin Group (NZ), cnr Airborne and Rosedale Roads, Albany, Auckland 1310, New Zealand (a division of Pearson New Zealand Ltd)

Penguin Books (South Africa) (Pty) Ltd, 24 Sturdee Avenue, Rosebank, Johannesburg 2196, South Africa

Penguin Books Ltd, Registered Offices: 80 Strand, London WC2R 0RL, England

Copyright © 2004 by Penguin Group (USA) Inc.

All rights reserved. No part of this book shall be reproduced, stored in a retrieval system, or transmitted by any means, electronic, mechanical, photo-copying, recording, or otherwise, without written permission from the pub-lisher. No patent liability is assumed with respect to the use of the information contained herein. Although every precaution has been taken in the preparation of this book, the publisher and author assume no responsibility for errors or omissions. Neither is any liability assumed for damages resulting from the use of information contained herein. For information, address Alpha Books, 800 East 96th Street, Indianapolis, IN 46240.

THE POCKET IDIOT'S GUIDE TO and Design are registered trademarks of Penguin Group (USA) Inc.

International Standard Book Number: 1-59257-355-X
Library of Congress Catalog Card Number: 2004115237

06   05   04   8   7   6   5   4   3   2   1

Interpretation of the printing code: The rightmost number of the first series of numbers is the year of the book's printing; the rightmost number of the second series of numbers is the number of the book's printing. For example, a printing code of 04-1 shows that the first printing occurred in 2004.

Printed in the United States of America

Note: This publication contains the opinions and ideas of its author. It is intended to provide helpful and informative material on the subject matter cov-ered. It is sold with the understanding that the author and publisher are not engaged in rendering professional services in the book. If the reader requires personal assistance or advice, a competent professional should be consulted.

The author and publisher specifically disclaim any responsibility for any liabil-ity, loss, or risk, personal or otherwise, which is incurred as a consequence, directly or indirectly, of the use and application of any of the contents of this book.

Most Alpha books are available at special quantity discounts for bulk purchases for sales promotions, premiums, fund-raising, or educational use. Special books, or book excerpts, can also be created to fit specific needs.

For details, write: Special Markets, Alpha Books, 375 Hudson Street, New York, NY 10014.

Contents

Appendixes

Introduction

Shopping for an annuity these days is a lot like going to look for a new car. Over here are the minivans, slow, but safe and predictable; next to them are the SUVs, faster and sportier, but okay to get the kids to soccer practice; and then there are the sports cars—fast, sleek, and built with risk in mind.

How do you choose? Which one is right for you? Okay, I'm not going to beat the car shopping analogy to death, but two similarities are worth pursuing. Both purchases involve large sums of money and some complicated information to digest.

That's where this book can help—at least, with the annuities. I cover the basics of annuities and go into some detail on the three different types—ranging from conservative and predictable to letting it ride on the stock market. I spend a significant amount of time on variable annuities because they are the hottest product on the market and the most complicated. Unfortunately, unscrupulous financial professionals have encouraged people to invest in variable annuities who had no business putting money in this product.

This book is not about why you should or should not invest in annuities. It is about understanding annuities. I wrote it with the belief that you can make your own decision once you have the information you need.

Extras

Look for these sidebars throughout the book—
they contain important concepts and bits of information that will help you better understand
annuities.

Careful _____

These give you a heads-up on what to
watch out for when considering an annuity
investment.

Consider This _____

These give you bits of information to
consider when thinking about annuities.

Financial Speak _____

These define financial terms important to
understanding annuities.

It's Your Money _____

These are financial tips that you will
want to mull over; after all, it is *your*
money.

Acknowledgments

Thanks, once again, to my wife, Cyndy, for taking up the slack as I let my chores slide while working on this book. My youngest daughter, Emma, age 7, was very understanding when Daddy needed to work. Writing books is hard work on the family, too.

Thanks also to Paul Dinas at Alpha Books for the opportunity to do another book with this fine group, and another chance to work with development editor Nancy Lewis, who has guided me through other projects.

Special Thanks to the Technical Reviewer

The Complete Idiot's Guide to Annuities was reviewed by an expert who double-checked the accuracy of what you'll learn here, to help us ensure that this book gives you everything you need to know about annuities. Special thanks are extended to Ken Kaplan.

Trademarks

All terms mentioned in this book that are known to be or are suspected of being trademarks or service marks have been appropriately capitalized. Alpha Books and Penguin Group (USA) Inc. cannot attest to the accuracy of this information. Use of a term in this book should not be regarded as affecting the validity of any trademark or service mark.

Chapter 1

The ABCs of Annuities

In This Chapter

- What are annuities?
- Types of annuities
- Phases of an annuity
- Comparing qualified and nonqualified annuities

First the good news. Thanks to advances in medical science, we are living longer, more active lives. Now the bad news. Thanks to advances in medical science, we are living longer, more active lives. Why is that bad news, you ask? Because our retirement nest egg may not live as long as we do. In other words, many of us approaching retirement are in danger of outliving our money.

You've probably heard stories in the news media about the troubles facing social security and Medicare as tens of millions of baby boomers approach retirement. Both programs seem to be teetering on the brink of collapse as more people draw from them and fewer contribute. Will there be anything left for you?

Did the stock market meltdown following the boom of the late 1990s turn your 401(k) into a 201(k) or worse? Maybe you are ready to retire now or in the near future—what are your options? How can you make sure you don't "outlive" your money?

Here's some closing good news: For some people, an annuity can provide an additional means of saving for retirement with special features, like a guaranteed lifetime income, that are not found in other financial products.

This chapter gives a broad overview of annuities as an introduction to the several different types and kinds. Consider this the "10,000-foot view" of the topic and the introduction of some basic terms that will prove useful in later chapters as we dig deeper into annuities.

Taking Out a Contract

The first thing you should know about an annuity is that it represents a contract between you and a life insurance company. The life insurance company obligates itself to pay you either immediately or at some future date a fixed amount of money or an amount to be determined for an agreed-upon period, based on your contribution to the contract. It is important to note that you "buy" the contract rather than "invest" in the life insurance company or a marketable security—annuities are not securities.

For the most conservative annuity contracts, this
means the insurance company bears the investment
and market risk. If you buy one annuity that guarantees 6 percent interest for six years, the life
insurance company must pay that interest rate
regardless of market conditions or interest rates.

Why Life Insurance Companies?

Life insurance companies sell annuities because
they carry a death benefit on the life of the owner.
In addition, some payment options for annuities
are based on the life expectancy of the *annuitant*.

$ Financial Speak

An **annuitant** is the person the life insurance company uses to base annuity payments on. Some payout options are for the
life of the annuitant, so the life insurance
company estimates the life expectancy of the
annuitant and divides the payments to cover
that term. The owner of the annuity does not
have to be the annuitant, but it usually is.

The annuitant and owner of the annuity are usually
the same person, but not necessarily. In this book, I
assume that the annuitant and owner are the same
person unless I state otherwise. The other named
party in the contract is the beneficiary. When the
owner dies, the beneficiary receives the death benefit (if any). If the annuity names no beneficiary, the
benefit goes to the owner's estate.

One other term you'll hear in this book and any time you talk to a financial professional about annuities is *premium*. That's probably a familiar term to you. You see it every time you open a bill from the insurance company for your auto, homeowners, or life insurance. It's what you pay for insurance. As you might guess, *premium* refers to the money you contribute to the annuity, but don't let it confuse you; annuities are not insurance policies.

Value of "Guarantee"

The death benefit, which we discuss in more detail shortly, provides a "guarantee" that is unique among privately sponsored financial products. For most annuities, if you die while the death benefit is in effect, your heirs receive at least what you have invested, plus any appreciation (minus any withdrawals you have made).

The issuing life insurance company backs the payout options offered through annuities, so it is important to deal with a reputable firm. For the most part, individual states regulate life insurance companies, which means 50 different sets of rules and regulations.

It also means that your cousin in California may have an annuity with a feature that is not available to you in Virginia, for example. I have covered the basics in this book, but I can't account for all of the minute differences in the 50 states.

Your best bet is to deal with life insurance companies that are highly rated by the two major rating agencies, A. M. Best and Standard & Poor's (S&P). Look for an A. M. Best rating of A- or better and an S&P rating of AA or better with a "positive" or "stable" outlook notation. Another rating company is Moody's, but it rates only insurance companies that request it, so you won't find every firm listed with it. You can find an explanation of each company's ratings at www.annuities-central.com/financial_ratings_for_annuities.html.

Specific safeguards are in place to protect annuity owners, but it never hurts to stick with the higher-rated companies, especially when it comes to variable annuities.

Although basic annuities are conservative investments, they are not as safe as similar savings products. The Federal Deposit Insurance Corp. (FDIC) insures bank certificates of deposit for up to $100,000, in case the bank folds. The U.S. government backs Treasury bonds and bills with its full faith and credit.

Annuity Contracts

Annuities come in three types: fixed, equity-indexed, and variable. They differ primarily in how they create future value, and they range from the most conservative (fixed) to the most aggressive (variable). Here is a quick look at how they are the same and how they differ.

Fixed Annuity

Fixed annuities are the simplest and most widely used of all annuities. They look very much like a bank certificate of deposit or bond, but they act differently and have extra bells and whistles.

A fixed annuity guarantees you an interest rate for a specified period while you are accumulating money and guarantees a payout of a specific amount over a certain period.

For example, if you purchased a six-year fixed annuity paying 4.3 percent, the issuing life insurance company would guarantee that rate for six years. At the end of six years, you could choose another guarantee period, depending on what was offered, or the annuity would continue to earn interest at whatever interest rate the company was offering.

This is just one example of one product. Although fixed annuities are very simple, there are many variations and combinations of guarantee periods, minimum investment requirements, and other variables.

Equity-Indexed Annuity

An equity-indexed annuity is a fixed annuity with an interest kicker tied to one of the major stock indexes, such as the S&P 500 Index. An interest kicker allows you to earn extra interest on your account if the performance of the index does well. The product is more aggressive than a simple fixed annuity, but less risky than a variable annuity.

Equity-indexed annuities vary widely. They offer a minimal guaranteed interest rate over a specified term. The contract also calls for additional interest or value, based on the change in the value of the index tied to the product.

For example, a contract might call for a five-year guaranteed interest rate of 3 percent. The contract might also specify the percentage difference between the values of the S&P 500 Index on the beginning and ending dates of the contract. A predetermined formula applies this value to the contract. If the underlying index is flat or loses value, the contract does not lose money.

Variable Annuity

When it comes to interest and controversy, the variable annuity is the unchallenged champion. With variable annuities, you give up a guaranteed return for the opportunity to participate in stock market returns that may or may not exceed what a regular fixed annuity would have provided.

A variable annuity is essentially a fixed annuity wrapped around a group of mutual funds, called *subaccounts.*

($) Financial Speak _____

Subaccounts are really mutual funds in which you invest your money in a variable annuity. Professional managers handle them separately from the life insurance company, and the Securities and Exchange Commission (SEC), among others, regulates them.

The big catch with variable annuities is that you don't know what the value of your contract is because it will fluctuate based on how well the sub-accounts you pick do in the market.

Unlike other annuities, you can lose your premium, just as you can in the regular market. The only way you can recoup your premium in a losing position before you begin withdrawals is to die, in which case your heirs get your premium as a death bene-fit. Of course, that's a tough way to get even.

The upside is, in a rising market, you can do very well because of the tax-deferred growth. This and some other trading features make variable annuities very attractive to many people, despite high fees and other drawbacks that we get into in Chap-ters 6, 7, and 8.

Annuity Payouts

Previously, I said that the *type* of annuity was deter-mined by how the contract created value. When it comes to defining the *kind* of annuity, we look at when the payout occurs: We have immediate and deferred annuities.

Immediate Annuity

As the name suggests, an immediate annuity is one that begins paying immediately or within one year of purchase. There is usually no waiting for pay-ments to begin, unless the owner structures the payout that way.

The insurance company agrees to pay you a specified sum for the rest of your life or for a certain period in exchange for a lump-sum contribution or premium. You, the owner, give up your right to ever get back your premium in a lump sum. In other words, once the payouts start, there's no going back.

It's Your Money

The market for annuities is very competitive. Life insurance companies compete for your business with attractive rates and special features. With a little digging, it is possible to find an annuity with just the right mix of features to fit your individual need.

I said earlier that the lifetime income was one of the most attractive features of an annuity. Here is the practical reality of that benefit. If you buy an immediate annuity and select the lifetime income payout, the insurance company estimates your life expectancy and begins paying you a monthly (if that's the frequency you pick) sum that will retire your premium over your expected lifespan.

If the insurance company expects you to live 20 more years and you fool them and live 30 more years, they still have to pay the same amount every month for the extra 10 years. However, (heaven forbid) if you live only 10 more years, they put the balance of your premium in their pocket unless the contract continues the death benefit or you select a death benefit option.

Deferred Annuity

Deferred annuities are contracts that provide a payout at some future date—at least one year beyond the purchase date. People use deferred annuities in retirement planning either to postpone the payout to a time after retirement or to allow time to fund the annuity through periodic contributions. No matter how you fund it, if you aren't going to withdraw money anytime soon, it's a deferred annuity.

During this time, your contributions and earnings grow tax-deferred until you begin withdrawals. This is one of the biggest selling points of annuities.

When you are ready to begin withdrawing money from the deferred annuity, you convert it into an immediate annuity. The main difference is that, in most contracts, when you begin payments or annuitization, the death benefit ends unless you choose one of the available options, depending on the individual contract.

All three types of annuities (fixed, equity-indexed, and variable) can be either deferred or immediate, depending on when the payout begins.

Annuity Phases

All three types of annuities have two phases: the accumulation and the payout.

The accumulation phase is the time when you are saving for retirement. It corresponds to a deferred annuity. During this phase, your premium and earnings are growing in a tax-deferred contract; the death benefit also is in effect.

During the payout phase, you begin receiving payments from the annuity. You can choose from a wide variety of options, so your decision deserves careful consideration—in most cases, once you choose a course of payment, you cannot change it.

If these two phases seem vaguely like the two types of annuities (deferred and immediate), don't be surprised or confused. There are some good reasons for distinguishing between the two phases.

It's Your Money

It is also important to note that once the payout phase begins, the death benefit (often touted in annuity advertisements) ends, with the exception of certain payout and death benefit options. Like options you add on a new car, they come with a price.

Death Benefit

Another one of the main attributes of annuities is the so-called death benefit. The life insurance company touts this provision—which you pay for, by the way—as protection for your estate against a loss of premium in the event of your untimely death.

The insurance part of annuities is a policy on the life of the owner that accompanies each annuity during the accumulation phase. It is not something the insurance company offers out of the goodness of its heart; companies build the fee into all annuities.

The death benefit usually guarantees that if the owner dies during the accumulation phase, the named beneficiary receives the value of the contract or the premium invested, whichever is greater. For fixed annuities, the value of the contract should always be more than the premium invested. For equity-indexed annuities, the premium invested might be greater, but most with a guaranteed minimum interest rate should have a higher contract value. With variable annuities, the premium invested might exceed the value of the contract if the subaccounts have lost money.

Careful

As attractive as the death benefit seems, studies show that it comes into play on very few annuities. Carefully consider the expense when deciding whether you need a higher death benefit.

Qualified vs. Nonqualified

Annuities are primarily retirement savings tools. In this capacity, you can use them either within or outside qualified retirement plans. In either case, annuities have some attractive features for retirement planning. I cover the tax consequences in more detail in Chapter 5.

A qualified retirement plan is one approved by the IRS for special tax treatment of your money. IRAs and 401(k) plans are examples of qualified plans.

In both cases, you can contribute pretax dollars to these plans (with the exception of the Roth IRA). You don't pay income tax on your contribution, so you lower your current tax obligation. While the money remains in the plan, it earns interest in a tax-deferred environment, which means you don't owe income or other taxes on any profits. Instead, when you withdraw money during your retirement, you may pay taxes on the full amount.

Qualified retirement plans have a number of restrictions regarding how much you can contribute, when you can withdraw your funds, when you must withdraw your funds, and other rules. If you fail to follow the rules, you may face heavy penalties from the IRS.

Annuities outside established retirement plans are nonqualified for tax purposes. This means the money you contribute is after-tax dollars. Your contribution grows tax-deferred while in the annuity, so there are no tax bills until you begin the payout phase.

What Are the Limits?

Qualified retirement plans place limits on how much you can contribute each year. For example, traditional IRAs have a $4,000 limit, with a $500 catch-up bonus for people age 50 and over for the calendar year 2005. That is all you can contribute, assuming you meet the income and other guidelines. If you use an annuity for your IRA, you are bound to these restrictions.

However, the unqualified annuity is unrestricted in how much you can contribute, although some insurance companies place limits on the size they will take. This is a major advantage for some people who have maxed out traditional qualified savings programs. If you have a big chunk of cash from an inheritance or the sale of a business, you won't have any problem finding a life insurance company willing to sell you an annuity for just about any amount.

Retirement Planning

Many people of all ages, but especially those approaching retirement in the next 10 years or so, are not feeling so confident about being able to afford the kind of lifestyle they hope to enjoy.

The rising costs of health care alone are enough to frighten many of us into rethinking when we are going to retire, not to mention how much more expensive everything is.

Annuities may be the answer for some people looking to sock away more money for retirement in a tax-deferred environment. With virtually no limit on contributions and a wide variety of products to choose from, annuities may just be the ticket for supplementing your retirement plan.

Benefits of Tax-Deferred

The benefit of tax-deferred savings is significant. When your money is growing in this sheltered environment, it compounds faster and you don't get any nasty tax bills at the end of the year.

What difference does it make in dollars and cents? Let's look at two identical investments of $10,000. One account is a taxable account, and the other is a tax-deferred annuity. Both pay 6 percent annually. You pay 30 percent in income taxes. At the end of six years, the taxable account is worth $12,800. The annuity is valued at $14,185—a difference of $1,385.

Of course, you will still owe tax on the profit of $4,185 when you withdraw it—no avoiding taxes forever, but better later when you may be in a lower tax bracket than sooner.

Creditor Protected

One of the more obscure benefits of annuities is available in only a handful of states and involves protection of assets in annuities from creditors.

For people in professions that attract lawsuits (some physicians, for example), socking away cash in annuities may provide protection from creditors in some cases. I strongly encourage anyone considering purchasing an annuity for this type of protection to seek competent legal counsel before making the purchase. This is a complicated area of law that only an attorney should address. Don't accept an answer from a life insurance company salesperson.

The Least You Need to Know

- Annuities are a contract between you and an insurance company.

- Annuities come in three types: fixed, equity-indexed, and variable.

- There are also two kinds of annuities: immediate and deferred.

- The death benefit usually pays the beneficiary the greater of the premium invested or the contract value.

- Annuities allow your savings to grow tax-deferred. You pay taxes only when you begin making withdrawals.

Chapter 2

Gathering Your Coins

In This Chapter

- Annuities and your portfolio
- The accumulation phase
- Qualified and nonqualified annuities explained
- Contribution limits

In this chapter, we discuss the role of annuities in your overall financial plan and how they compare to other products.

Annuities are among the most flexible financial products on the market, but for a variety of reasons, they have never really caught the public's imagination the way other products have. You won't often hear someone whispering to a colleague that she has a "hot tip" on an annuity.

That raises an interesting point: Should you compare, for example, mutual fund returns and annuity yields? My answer is, no. The products serve two different purposes. Even though variable annuities attempt to combine the two products, they shouldn't be confused.

In this chapter, we also look at how you might fund an annuity, how contributions for qualified and nonqualified annuities differ, and some appropriate and inappropriate uses of annuities in retirement plans.

Annuities in Your Portfolio

One of the arguments you might hear against annuities is "You can do better with mutual funds." Really? These blanket statements always amuse me because they presume that throwing money at any mutual fund will earn a profit. You know that is not true.

The more correct statement is that, over the long term, an investment in a portfolio representative of the overall stock market has earned an average return of 10 to 12 percent annually, depending on how you calculate returns.

Despite this well-qualified statement, your potential for higher returns is in the market, not in annuities, although variable annuities attempt to mitigate this advantage. Let's look at the difference between investing and saving, and how those concepts apply to annuities.

The Role of Investing

Typical annuity buyers are at or approaching retirement age. They are still building a nest egg, however, and must guard against losing ground, so they avoid risky investments.

The role of investing for these people is to continue building capital and to protect against inflation. Although inflation has not been a problem for several years, even a small rate continually eats away at your nest egg.

For example, if you had buried $100,000 in your backyard in 1994 with the plan that you would dig it up in 2004 when you retired, you would get a nasty shock. Even though inflation was relatively low during this period, your $100,000 would have shrunk considerably. Thanks to inflation, what cost $100,000 in 1994 is price-tagged at $126,382.27 in 2004. Just to keep up with inflation, your investment would have needed to earn an after-tax return to compensate for an average 2.64 percent loss each year due to inflation.

As you can see, there is a need for investments that will earn enough to outpace the combined drags of taxes and inflation, even into retirement years. But this doesn't mean chasing high-risk technology stocks or "the next big thing."

A balanced portfolio that takes into consideration your time horizon, risk tolerance, and financial goals will achieve the desired results of building or replenishing your nest egg, given enough time. However, riding the market through its inevitable ups and downs can be a troubling experience.

What if you need to access your nest egg during one of the periods when the stock market is contracting? The one situation you want to avoid is selling low—that is, divesting a stock or mutual fund at its low point just to free some cash for living expenses. Here is where savings can help.

The Role of Savings

The role of savings for typical annuity buyers at or approaching retirement is to protect capital. These people want to preserve and protect what they have accumulated. In addition, savings provide a source of liquidity to fund everyday expenses once their working income stops.

A number of products are available for this purpose, including bank CDs, bonds, money market mutual funds, mattresses, cans buried in the backyard, and so on. Annuities—especially fixed annuities—certainly belong in this category. In general, they all provide a predictable rate of return that may not beat inflation and taxes, but they won't be too far behind. Even if they are falling behind, retirees are more concerned with predictability than "beating the market" with their savings.

Retirees still want some assets in the market, to protect against inflation and allow for some more growth. However, they should start shifting assets into more stable, fixed-income investments, which will soften any wild swings in the market and provide more stability to their portfolio. Annuities, along with bonds and bond mutual funds, offer the kind of predictability and stability many retirees find helpful.

 Consider This

> Retirees or near-retirees need to focus on preservation of their capital because their working years are over and it can be difficult to recover lost ground from an investment strategy gone bad.

Annuities: Investing or Saving?

So, do you invest in annuities or save with annuities? Does anyone care? Although it may seem like splitting semantic hairs, there is a reason for spending a little time on this.

Fixed annuities are savings instruments, even though you may hear people talk about "investing" in annuities. Your expectation should be a stable return and payout, as you will learn in subsequent chapters.

Variable annuities are investments. You can lose money by investing in a variable annuity, but you can also earn substantially more than with a simple savings instrument.

Equity-indexed annuities straddle the fence between savings and investment instruments by combining some elements of both. With most contracts, there is a guaranteed minimum, usually 3 percent, and the possibility for gains approaching those at market levels. With these expectations in mind, we can move forward.

The Accumulation Phase

All annuities have an accumulation phase. Recall from Chapter 1 that deferred annuities postpone a payout for at least one year from the purchase date, while immediate annuities begin paying out immediately.

Obviously, the accumulation phase for an immediate annuity is short. You buy the annuity, and off you go. Things can drag out with the deferred annuity for some time.

Lump Sum

The most familiar way to fund an annuity is with a lump sum. Clearly, this is the way you fund an immediate annuity. Many fixed-annuity providers structure their products like CDs or bonds, partly so consumers will be comfortable with purchasing a familiar-looking product.

Where do consumers come up with the lumps? Very often, they are maturing CDs or bonds. Empty-nesters often sell their family home and "buy down" to a smaller home or condo and buy an annuity with the difference. Owners of certain life insurance policies with high cash values can roll some of those assets into an annuity in a tax-free exchange under certain circumstances. Retirees frequently find that many of the assets that were important when there were children in the house are no longer necessary.

A variety of pension and retirement plans may provide lump-sum settlements. A large *Roth IRA*, for example, is tax-free money that you can use to fund an annuity. In this case, you wouldn't be interested in deferring taxes because there are no taxes due, but you might be interested in guaranteeing an income stream for the rest of your life or utilizing one of the other payout strategies discussed in Chapter 3.

Financial Speak

The **Roth IRA** differs from a regular IRA in several ways. Chief among them is the fact that contributions are not tax-deductible; however, withdrawals are tax-free. There are income restrictions and withdrawal schedules.

Periodic Contributions

The other way to fund an annuity is through periodic contributions. Many annuities offer the option of opening the account with an initial deposit and then making periodic (usually monthly) contributions to the contract. Some even debit your checking account directly for the amount you authorize.

The initial amount varies from annuity to annuity, but it is usually higher than the small sums needed to open mutual fund accounts, for example. Be sure to read the contract information carefully so you understand how it works. They are all a little different.

For those who don't have lumps of cash lying around, this is a convenient and affordable way to purchase annuities. The downside is, the longer you take to fund the annuity, the less interest you earn. As you'll see later, some annuities offer a substantial bonus interest rate in the first year, to lure in dollars. If you choose to purchase such an annuity, you lose the benefit of that bonus if you can't drop a large sum in the first year.

Tax Breaks, Anyone?

Annuities come with built-in tax breaks. Your earnings grow tax-deferred as long as they stay in the annuity, which really speeds the compounding, as you saw in Chapter 1. Only when you withdraw cash must your profits face the taxman.

In Chapter 5, I discuss taxes in more detail; however, let me set up that discussion with some preliminary explanations of how the IRS treats money flowing into annuities for tax purposes.

Qualified Annuities

You may use annuities as vehicles for qualified retirement plans. The IRS requires retirement

plans to meet certain criteria before it certifies
the plan as qualified.

For our current discussion, we are concerned with
what happens to money flowing into qualified plans
and how that treatment applies to annuities.

IRAs, 401(k)s, and Others

You are probably familiar with IRA and 401(k)
retirement plans. You can use annuities in any
of these plans as a funding vehicle.

In the case of IRAs, you establish those individually, and you could certainly use annuities. Money
you use to fund the IRA is pretax because you get
to take a deduction on your individual income tax
for your contribution within the limits set by IRA
rules (except for Roth IRAs, which you fund with
after-tax dollars). IRA rules limit your contributions and set income restrictions.

It's Your Money _____

Recent changes in the rules governing
qualified retirement plans allow people
over the age of 50 to contribute more to
the plans. Called catch-up amounts, these
extra amounts acknowledge the fact that
many of us were slow in beginning to
save for retirement.

IRAs and most other qualified retirement plans
have withdrawal requirements that state when and

how much you must take out of the plan. Most annuity contracts don't have such restrictions, but when you use an annuity to fund a qualified plan, you must follow the rules of the qualified plan.

In addition to the traditional IRA and the Roth IRA, you can use annuities to fund a number of other IRA options, such as the SEP IRA (which is a retirement plan for self-employed people or owners of small companies that allows them to contribute to IRAs on behalf of employees, including themselves). In each case, the rules governing the particular IRA define the contribution limits and withdrawal time requirements.

403(b) Plans and Others

403(b) plans are very similar to 401(k) plans, but they are for government workers at the federal, state, and local levels and people working for nonprofit organizations.

For years, these folks were limited to basic annuities, called tax-sheltered annuities (TSAs) for their retirement investments. In recent years, the regulations covering 403(b) plans have become less restrictive.

Fixed annuities are appropriate for almost any retirement plan in which your goal is a stable return. However, you should always check fees and other expenses against other comparable products to determine the best choice for you.

Before Tax Contributions

One of the distinguishing features of qualified retirement plans is the treatment of contributions. The good news is you get to fund these plans with money before you pay taxes on it, which reduces your current income tax liability. The bad news is, when you take money out, you may pay taxes on every penny because no tax was ever paid.

Appropriate Annuity Products

Both fixed annuities and equity-indexed annuities are appropriate for qualified retirement plans. Fixed annuities fall into the more conservative category, while equity-indexed annuities are more risky, but not so far out there that they are inappropriate for retirement plans. As a savings component of your retirement plan, annuities work just fine. Normally, you gain nothing extra by using a tax-deferred product like annuities in qualified retirement plans—there is no such thing as double deferment. However, annuities can offer a competitive and important stable interest rate for your retirement planning.

Variable annuities, however, are not appropriate for qualified retirement plans. They are investment products and add nothing to a qualified retirement plan. The high fees associated with variable annuities make them uncompetitive in the qualified retirement market. You are better off investing directly in mutual funds and bypassing the expensive overhead of variable annuities for your qualified retirement plan.

Nonqualified Annuities

One of the great features of annuities is that they carry a tax benefit of their own, without the restrictions of a qualified retirement account.

All your earnings during the accumulation period grow in an environment sheltered from income or capital gains taxes. While there are some restrictions on annuities, they are mild compared to the rules imposed on qualified retirement plans. This is why many people turn to annuities to supplement their retirement plans.

Tax-Deferred Earnings

All your earnings in an annuity are tax-deferred until you begin to withdraw them. This feature is unique in comparable products with comparable returns. With no annual income or capital gains tax due, annuities' earnings grow faster than those of taxed products.

The Sky Is the Limit

Another feature that retirement planners like about annuities is that there is virtually no limit on the amount you can contribute. All qualified retirement plans have limits to the amount you can put in each year. These restrictions make it difficult to build a substantial nest egg or, if you are late getting started, accumulate any size of retirement account.

Your 401(k) at work may offer a *matching contribution* by your employer, but the law limits how much you can contribute. Once you max out your best options, you may still be short of your retirement goals. Of course, your employer may not offer a 401(k), 403(b), or other qualified retirement plan.

> **$ Financial Speak** _____
>
> If your employer offers a partial match to your 401(k) plan, known as a **matching contribution,** you should seriously consider investing up to at least the matching percentage. This is free money; don't leave it on the table. If you're not sure what the plan offers, check with the company's human resources department.

Regardless of your other options, you can purchase any annuity you want. If you want to buy a $100,000 annuity, you do not have to meet any income or other test from the IRS.

After Tax Contributions

All of the money you put into an annuity is after tax—that is, it does not result in a lower current income tax bill like most qualified retirement plans do.

You must weigh this drawback against the other benefits of annuities. As with all financial decisions, you should look at all of your options before deciding the best vehicles for your retirement dollars.

The Least You Need to Know

- Fixed annuities are savings instruments, while variable annuities are investments that can lose money. Equity-indexed annuities fall somewhere in between.

- You can fund an annuity in one lump sum or through a series of regular contributions.

- Fixed and equity-indexed annuities are suitable for the savings portion of qualified retirement plans, but variable annuities are not.

- Annuities' earnings are tax-deferred, and there is no limit to how much you can contribute to nonqualified annuities.

Chapter **3**

Reaping Your Rewards

In This Chapter

- How the payout phase works
- Single-life payout options
- Multiple-life payout options
- Systematic withdrawals

When it comes to taking money out of an annuity, you have more options than with any other financial instrument. That's one of the main benefits consumers find attractive.

The biggie, of course, is a guaranteed income for life. No other financial instrument can offer you this option. You don't have to take the payout as a lifetime income, but many annuity owners do choose this option.

You should be aware of a few limitations and cautions before you purchase an annuity, though. When payouts begin, the contract is annuitized—that is, a program of systematic payments is begun.

Once you start, you can't stop or reverse annuitization except by death.

Know Your Annuity

The whole idea of buying an annuity is to get to this point—an income stream in your retirement years. However, getting to the payout requires some preparation and planning.

I can't stress too strongly that not all annuities are the same. The annuities industry is very competitive, and life insurance companies offer annuities with many different features to appeal to as broad an audience as possible. Keep looking until you find the annuity with the features that fit your personal needs.

Not every annuity offers every payout option or death benefit discussed in this book. Some may offer ones I have not discussed. Be sure you understand the contract's exact features before you buy.

When You Can Start

We know that the rules of qualified retirement plans govern annuities in those plans regarding distributions. However, even nonqualified annuities have some restrictions on distributions.

Under normal circumstances, you can't begin distributions before age 59$^1/_2$, which is the same minimum age for qualified plans. There are exceptions for the disability or death of the owner.

If you begin distributions before age 59^1/$_2$, the IRS imposes a 10-percent penalty on any earnings in the annuity.

Unlike most qualified retirement plans, you generally do not have to begin taking distributions by any certain age, although some companies have a contract maturity age of 85 when they want you to begin. In many cases, you can change this age.

What About the Death Benefit?

As you'll see in the next chapter, there are many options to consider with the death benefit. However, when you are choosing a payout plan, consider the death benefit along with the payout.

Under some payout plans, the death benefit goes away as soon as you begin receiving payments or annuitize the contract. If the death benefit is important to you, make sure you know what happens to it under the payout plan you choose.

Factors to Consider

You can use the flexibility of annuities to structure a retirement income stream to meet your needs. By combining different payout scenarios, you can provide the income coverage necessary to support your retirement lifestyle.

For example, you may need more income in the early years of retirement, when you anticipate higher expenses, and less in later years. On the other hand, it may be more important for you to provide a secure income for your spouse, regardless of what happens to you. Annuity payout plans can accommodate all these factors and more.

Careful _____

> When planning your retirement, don't lock all of your assets into structures so tightly that you can't make major changes if you need to. Life has a way of happening to our best plans.

Types of Payouts

Payouts or distributions from annuities range from the simple single life to the complex multiple lives with several options. Each payout option is discussed in the sections that follow.

As a rule of thumb, the simpler the payout is, the higher the payout is; the more options you add, the lower the payout is.

Single Life

Single-life payouts consider only one person, the annuitant/owner, in figuring out what the monthly income will be from the payout. Whether there is a death benefit depends on the type of payout.

Lifetime Income

The lifetime income is the simplest payout option and offers one of the highest dollar amounts. Simply stated, the lifetime income payout guarantees you an income for the rest of your life, no matter how long or short your life is.

For example, if you choose this payout option at age 65, you receive an income stream (usually monthly, but some contracts pay semiannually or quarterly) for the rest of your life. If you live to be 85, 95, or 105, you still receive the same payment.

On the other hand, if you die at age 66, that's it—the insurance keeps the rest of your money because most single-lifetime income payouts carry no death benefit. Nothing passes to your heirs.

Refund Lifetime Income Annuity

A refund lifetime income annuity is the same as a simple lifetime income, except that if you die before withdrawing a sum equal to your original premium, your estate receives the difference.

For example, assume that you purchased a refund lifetime income annuity with a $100,000 premium and began withdrawing a monthly income through annuitization, but you died at age 70. If your withdrawals amounted to only $20,000, your estate would receive $80,000 either in a lump sum or in a continuation of your monthly income until your original premium was exhausted.

This option guarantees that either you or your heirs, not the life insurance company, will benefit from your original premium. Of course, this option comes with a price, in the form of lower monthly benefits to you.

> **It's Your Money** _____
>
> Payout options and other benefit options make annuities flexible and popular retirement tools, but very few are free. Choose only those options that you really need, to keep your return as high as possible.

Lifetime with Period Certain

Another variation of the lifetime income payout involves guaranteeing that payments will continue for a certain number of years, even if you die. This option usually is offered in five-year increments and might be stated like this: single life with X years certain. The X might be 5, 10, 15, or 20 years.

This payout guarantees a level income for your lifetime, but if you die before the X years certain are up, your beneficiary receives the remainder of the payments to complete the certain period.

For example, if you had a single life with 10 years certain payout and you died after 4 years, the beneficiary named in your annuity contract would receive the same payment for the remaining 6 years of the 10 years certain period.

More Than One Life

One of the uses of life insurance is to replace the
income stream of a spouse in the event of death.
The same benefit is available for annuities by
choosing the joint and survivor options.

These options consider the lives of both individuals
in calculating the monthly income stream and give
you some options regarding what happens if one
partner dies. The industry calls them joint and survivor, meaning that both share the benefit when
alive, and the surviving partner continues to enjoy
the benefit in some form after the other's death.

Joint and Survivor (100 Percent)

The joint and survivor payout recognizes the need
to continue an income stream after a spouse's
death. With the 100 percent option, the surviving
spouse continues to receive the same benefit as
before the other's death.

 Consider This _____

> When planning for a retirement with
> your spouse, always consider three scenar-
> ios: You both live, the husband dies, or the
> wife dies. Try to determine how your finan-
> cial needs change in each situation.

This option protects the surviving spouse in two
ways. First, it continues the income stream uninter-
rupted. Second, the benefit is not part of the

deceased's estate and is not subject to the complications of *probate*.

> **($) Financial Speak** _____
>
> **Probate** is the process by which an administrator or executor manages and distributes the property according to the terms of a deceased person's will.

Joint and Survivor (75 Percent ... 50 Percent) First or Either

This option reduces the payment to the surviving co-annuitant on the death of the other by the amount specified in the contract. It makes no difference who dies first.

You might use this payout option when there was sufficient insurance coverage on both to compensate for the reduced monthly payment.

If you choose this option, you will receive a higher monthly income than with the 100 percent option for both co-annuitants.

Joint and Survivor (75 Percent ... 50 Percent) Only Primary Annuitant

With this payout, there is a primary annuitant and a contingent annuitant (instead of co-annuitants). The contract reduces the monthly income only if the primary annuitant dies. If the contingent annuitant dies, there is no reduction in income.

A person concerned about a spouse's well-being might exercise this type of payout option to ensure that even after his or her death, the income would continue.

Adding Options

You can add refund and period certain options to the joint and survivor payouts.

For example, you might add a cash refund option to the joint and survivor (100 percent) payout. This option would pay your beneficiaries the difference in a lump sum between your initial premium and what you had received to date upon the death of both annuitants.

The installment option would continue the payments the co-annuitants were receiving at the time of the last one's death to the beneficiaries. These payments would continue until your beneficiaries received your original premium back.

Likewise, you can add period certain options to the joint and survivor payouts to ensure payments continue for a fixed period.

A Certain Amount of Time or Money

Another payout option you can use in retirement planning is to structure payments for a guaranteed period. This option, which I've shown can be attached to other payout plans, is also a standalone plan.

A less familiar payout option fixes the monthly income required. Based on prevailing interest rates, the life insurance company will sell you an annuity for the period required to meet your income requirement.

Fixed Period Certain

In some circumstances, it is important to guarantee an income stream for a certain period to cover a fixed expense or some other financial need. You can select a fixed period certain payout to guarantee that payments continue for a specified number of years.

For example, after your kids left home, you bought a smaller house. Instead of paying cash for the house, you invested the difference and carried a mortgage on the new home. Now at retirement, you still have 15 years left on the note. To ensure that you can always make the payments, you might buy an annuity that would pay enough to cover your mortgage payment with a period certain of 15 years.

This payout continues to your heirs if you die before the period certain is up. The downside of this payout is that when the period certain is up, so is your money. Be sure you understand and use this payout correctly.

Fixed Amount Certain

A fixed amount certain annuity is like working the problem backward. With this payout option, you know the monthly income you need and the amount of money you have to invest. You buy an annuity that will stretch those monthly payments as far as possible.

Annuity salespeople have calculators that can figure almost any scenario you need. Although many companies don't specifically sell a "fixed amount certain" annuity, they can achieve the same results with a few simulations on their computer.

Systematic Withdrawals

I noted previously that once you annuitized a contract, the decision was irreversible. This is a problem for some people and in some circumstances. Systematic withdrawals are a way to establish a payout plan without locking yourself into a fixed schedule.

Many companies allow systematic withdrawals as an option on their annuities. Here's how it works: You establish a regular withdrawal pattern that fits your needs and the company's guidelines. During months when you don't need as much income, you can skip a payout or take a reduced one. Other times, you may need to take out more.

The flexibility to adjust payments and timing is appealing to many contract owners. Of course, there are some negatives.

For one thing, the IRS treats the first dollars you withdraw as earnings, so you pay taxes on everything you withdraw until you are down to your principal. This is not as attractive as spreading your tax liability over years under a normal annuitization.

Second, there is no income guarantee. If you burn up your money too quickly, too bad.

Estimates of Annuity Payouts

The following estimates show what various payout options might yield on a fixed annuity. The annuity premium is $100,000 for a 65-year-old man in Wisconsin. The numbers are illustrations only and do not reflect payouts from any individual company. The purpose of this illustration is to show the differences in dollar amounts.

Single Lifetime: $658. This is the simplest life annuitization and the one that pays the most. You will receive this monthly payment for the rest of your life, but when you die, the payments end and nothing goes to your beneficiary.

Single Lifetime Income with Up to 10 Years Guaranteed: $634. This annuitization guarantees that you will never outlive the income and provides something for your beneficiaries if you die in the first 10 years. The contract continues payments to your beneficiary through the tenth year.

Single Lifetime Income with Up to 20 Years Guaranteed: $583. This is the same as the previous option, except that the period is 20 years.

Guaranteed for Five-Year Period Certain Only: $1,777. This annuitization pays out over a five-year period. At the end of the five years, it completely depletes the account. If you die before five years is up, your beneficiary continues to receive payments through the end of the contract.

Guaranteed Income for 10-Year Period Certain Only: $978. This option is the same as the previous one, except that the period is 10 years.

Guaranteed Income for 15-Year Period Certain Only: $768. This option is the same as the previous one, except that the period is 15 years.

Guaranteed Income for 20-Year Period Certain Only: $644. This option is the same as the previous one, except that the period is 20 years.

You can get your own estimates by using the free calculator at www.immediateannuities.com.

Odds and Ends

So many options exist with annuities that it's hard to get your arms around all of them. If you shop for annuities for any length of time, you will probably stumble across some I haven't covered here, simply because life insurance companies are constantly thinking of new ways to package their products.

Partial Withdrawals

During the accumulation phase, you can withdraw or surrender for cash your annuity anytime you want. However, you may pay a stiff surrender charge for the privilege, and if you're younger than 59½, the IRS will take an additional 10 percent penalty.

Many annuities allow you to withdraw a certain percentage, often up to 10 percent, during this period without a surrender charge. (Unfortunately, the IRS isn't so forgiving.) Read your contract carefully to avoid extra charges. However, it's best to avoid all withdrawals unless you absolutely need the money. Annuities are long-term solutions, and you shouldn't tamper with them except in emergencies.

Emergencies

Speaking of emergencies, your annuity contract may allow withdrawals without penalty in the event of disability, confinement to a nursing home, terminal illness, or other major life event. Your contract will spell out those circumstances. The IRS is not so forgiving; however, you may get stuck with an early withdrawal penalty if you are under 59½.

 **Careful**

> Read your contract very carefully so you understand what it considers an emergency. If there is a possibility that you may need to withdraw your money, know what is required to avoid any big surrender charges.

Charitable Giving

Annuities make wonderful gifts for your favorite charity. I include charitable giving in the payout section because there are several ways you can receive an income from an annuity you have left in a charitable remaining trust or other trust vehicle.

Churches, educational institutions, nonprofit groups, and others are more than happy to show you how charitable giving works. However, trusts are complicated matters best discussed with a knowledgeable financial or legal adviser.

Who Guarantees the Payout?

It is a real benefit to have a large number of payout options, but what assurance do you have that your money will be available when you need it? Unlike most bank accounts, annuities are not insured by the FDIC and are not backed by the "full faith and credit of the U.S. Government," like U.S. Treasury issues.

Your annuity contract is only as good as the insurance company that wrote it. That's why it is important to pay attention to the underwriting company when purchasing an annuity.

The law requires insurance companies to keep separate reserves equal to the surrender value of all the annuity contracts it issues. The surrender value is the amount you would receive if you withdrew your entire principal out of your annuity, plus any earned interest and minus any withdrawals and surrender charges (if any).

Individual states may have additional restrictions. These reserves are not the same reserves the insurance company keeps to cover its life insurance policies.

Just because the law requires certain reserves doesn't mean every life insurance company is equal in terms of its ability to provide the payout when you need it. Remember, annuities are long-term contracts. If you choose a lifetime payout option, you are counting on a company to send you a check every month for the rest of your life, which could be (you hope) many years to come.

Refer to the section "Value of 'Guarantee'" in Chapter 1 for information on life insurance company–rating agencies.

The Least You Need to Know

- Annuities offer a wide variety of payouts to fit many financial needs.
- Payouts come in single- and multiple-life formats for specific retirement and survivor planning.
- You can structure payouts to fit specific periods or to refresh your original principal.
- Your annuity is only as good as the financial strength of the life insurance company that sold it.

Chapter 4

The Death Benefit

In This Chapter

- What life insurance adds
- Optional death benefits
- How annuities avoid probate
- Death benefit pros and cons

The old joke about life insurance is "You have to die to win"—not a rousing endorsement for a product that plays an important role in every family's financial plan.

How does life insurance make annuities different from other financial products? In this chapter, I discuss the pros and cons of life insurance and what it adds to annuities.

The death benefit in simple fixed annuities is not such a big deal, but it is still unique in the financial market. Where the death benefit really makes a difference is in variable annuities. How about investing in the stock market with no worry of losing money? There is a small catch (you have to die first), but that's what life insurance does for this product.

What Life Insurance Adds

Salespeople often talk about "guaranteed" returns and safety for your estate during their pitch. Life insurance is one part of the support that provides these assurances.

The ultimate security of your annuity always rests on the quality of the life insurance company selling the contract. That's how you protect yourself. The insurance company offers death benefit protection by doing what it does best and issuing an insurance policy on the annuity owner's life—for a fee, of course.

"Guaranteed" Returns

The industry applies the term *guaranteed* to two different aspects of annuities. First, marketing materials use it in connection with the interest rate paid by fixed annuities and a minimum interest rate paid by equity-indexed and the fixed-interest subaccount of variable annuities.

Fixed annuities often have a guaranteed interest rate for a certain period. After that, either the interest rate floats or the customer has other options, which I discuss in later chapters.

However, the guarantee we're interested in is the death benefit guarantee. Unless specifically excluded, all deferred annuities carry a death benefit during the accumulation phase. This benefit says that if you die during the accumulation phase, your beneficiary receives the greater of the following:

- Your contributions, minus any withdrawals
- The value of your account

For fixed annuities, this is a simple, straightforward benefit. However, for variable annuities, the death benefit may have some real value.

For example, if you were in the accumulation phase of a variable annuity and the market took a turn for the worse, you could lose a significant amount from your account. Your investments to date might have been $80,000, but the bad market made your account worth only $70,000. If you died at this point, your beneficiary would receive $80,000 (minus fees), assuming you had made no withdrawals.

Security for Heirs

How much value you place on the death benefit depends, in part, on how much importance you place on building an estate to pass on to your heirs.

Are you the type of person who says "I'm spending my kids' inheritance," or do you want to pass something along to your children or perhaps a favorite nonprofit group or church?

Even if you fall into the first group, most of us don't want to leave things in a mess that causes a financial hardship on those we leave behind.

Consider This _____

> Estate planning is a complex process if you have significant assets. Even with a more modest estate, you may want to employ a qualified estate attorney or planner to help you arrange matters.

Cash for Beneficiary

One of the general benefits of annuities augmented by the death benefit is that your beneficiary has almost immediate access to the annuity.

Depending on which phase the annuity was in at the time of the owner's death, the beneficiary may receive a cash settlement or a continuation of payments. It all depends on the original contract.

Annuities are not part of the estate and probate process, which means they may be quick sources of cash to help settle matters.

When the Death Benefit Ends

In some situations, the death benefit ends. For example, if the owner chooses a single-life payout, he can receive the maximum payment by forgoing the death benefit when payments begin. In this case, if the annuity owner dies after payments begin, the beneficiary gets nothing.

It is important that you completely understand the terms and conditions of the death benefit of any annuity before you buy. Annuity providers offer a wide variety of options; with a little shopping, you can find one with the combination of features you want.

Optional Death Benefits: Step-Ups

Like buying a new car and adding on those extras, you can enhance and customize many annuity contracts with optional death benefits. For the most part, these enhancements make sense only for variable annuities and, to a lesser extent, equity-indexed annuities. Fixed annuities don't need a stepped-up benefit because the value of the contract will never go down, which can happen with variable annuities and equity-indexed annuities.

The industry is constantly evolving, so you might discover an annuity with slightly different spins on these options or even some new options not listed here. The important point is to evaluate each option relative to your personal situation and make an informed decision.

The usual minimum death benefit for annuities returns the premium (minus withdrawals) if death occurs before the payout begins. This is good protection for owners of a variable annuity if the market goes against them just before their death, but what if they are doing great and their account is worth much more than the premium?

A step-up benefit allows you to lock in investment gains so that if you die, those gains pass to your beneficiaries.

> **It's Your Money** _____
>
> If your goal with investing in a variable annuity is to generate retirement income, forget the fancy death benefit options. Those extra fees are a drag on returns.

Annual Step-Up

An annual step-up death benefit increases the annuity owner's coverage to the highest value in any one year to lock in investment gains.

For example, if your premium to date is $150,000, but thanks to a roaring bull market, your account is worth $175,000, your death benefit is $175,000 to protect those gains. If the market retreats, your death benefit is still $175,000.

This coverage puts a floor under your gains, but it is expensive. Carefully consider the costs before selecting this option.

Percentage Step-Up

A percentage step-up death benefit option applies a percentage increase to your contributions each year. This is one way to hedge against inflation, but it also comes with a price.

If the market does well—or even mediocre—this benefit may be wasted on an account value that is larger than your premium plus the percentage increase (minus the fees, of course).

Every *X* Number of Years Step-Up

This option allows you to pick a number of years to periodically step up the death benefit (if the account value is high). You might choose every three years, for example, to look at the value. If it is higher than your contributions, you can step up the death benefit to that level, and it stays there, even if the account value falls later.

This is another way to protect account gains, but if your gains fall in an off year and then retreat during your option year, you may miss the opportunity.

Fees

Death benefits and the options don't come free. What you pay depends on several factors, but you *will* pay. Remember, the life insurance company is taking out a policy on you, and that policy has a premium.

How much? That is an excellent question to ask before buying any annuity product. Fees can be a major drain on your return, so you want to keep them as low as possible. Make sure that what you are getting in exchange for the fee is worth the drag on earnings.

It wouldn't be surprising to find death benefit fees (called mortality expenses) alone running 1.1 percent and higher. If you add some of the optional death benefits discussed previously, the fee might approach 1.75 percent.

For discussion purposes, say the mortality expense on an annuity was 1.25 percent. That means on a $200,000 account, the life insurance company will deduct $2,500 per year. That's a significant drain on your account's value—and there are other fees as well.

Death Benefit Summary

Salespeople often cite the death benefit as one of the main reasons to choose an annuity over another investment or savings instrument. Critics say the high fees and questionable value of the death benefit make annuities, especially variable annuities, a bad deal.

Here are views of the death benefit from both sides.

Death Benefit: Pro

Insurance is one of those things in life that no one enjoys paying for, but everyone is glad they have if they need it. Most people never have their house destroyed, but they would not miss a homeowner's insurance payment.

That's one way to approach the death benefit with annuities. You hope you don't need it, but you might be willing to pay the price to make sure it's there just in case.

These folks may want to pass on as much to beneficiaries as possible. They could be in poor health and are uninsurable in the open market for life insurance.

Whatever the reason, they are more interested in the security that insurance provides, despite the fact that, in most cases, the account value will exceed the premium, so there will be no loss to the heirs.

However, all potential annuity owners should have a clear idea of what they want to accomplish. This will guide them in deciding what to do about the death benefit and its options.

> **It's Your Money** _____
>
> Death benefit options are only one factor in variable annuities. If you invest in variable annuities, you need to consider the benefits and costs associated with the options available.

Death Benefit: Con

Do you really need or want the death benefit? Can you afford it? Detractors of variable annuities often ask this question right before telling you how much better off you would be with just mutual funds.

It is hard to argue with them that the death benefits aren't expensive. In our earlier example, the death benefit on a $200,000 account would cost $2,500 per year, which comes out to about $210 per month. A quick look on the Internet will find many quotes for $200,000 of term insurance for a lot less than $210 per month for a healthy man at age 65.

Besides, if your spouse is still alive (and unless you designate otherwise) upon your death, he or she becomes the new owner exactly where you were in the contract. That happens automatically and without insurance.

Death causes the surrender of less than 0.05 percent of all annuities, according to industry figures, which seems to suggest that people may be paying for unneeded protection.

> ### It's Your Money
>
> Security is one of the main reasons people buy annuities and are willing to give up the potentially higher returns they might find in other products. That is a perfectly legitimate reason for buying an annuity.

The Least You Need to Know

- The death benefit ensures that the beneficiary receives at least the premium, minus withdrawals.
- The death benefit is not part of the estate and goes directly to the heirs, avoiding probate.
- Optional death benefits allow you to extend the coverage, for a fee.
- Fees associated with the death benefit and options are significant.

Chapter **5**

A Taxing Concern

In This Chapter

- Tax consequences for nonqualified annuities
- Tax consequences for qualified annuities
- How distributions are taxed
- 1035 transfers

Annuities offer a deferral of taxes until you begin withdrawing money—then you must pay up. The deferral of taxes during the accumulation phase allows your account to grow much faster than regular accounts subject to yearly tax bills.

With nonqualified annuities, you don't get any break on your contributions, but contributions to qualified annuities do help with current income taxes.

However, the time comes when you start withdrawing money from your account, and the IRS is going to want a piece of it. In fact, they are going to want a big piece of it, which is one of the main complaints you'll hear about annuities, especially variable annuities.

Nonqualified Annuity Taxes

Nonqualified annuities are the weapon of choice for many people looking to save more for their retirement than allowed under typical qualified retirement plans.

Tax-deferred growth, guaranteed interest rates, flexible payout plans, and optional death benefits make annuities an attractive choice for funding your retirement. Why then, do some financial experts dislike them so? The answer is, in a word, *taxes*.

No Deduction for Contributions

For nonqualified annuities, the rough tax treatment begins at the funding stage. The IRS does not allow any deductions against current income for contributions to a nonqualified annuity.

For this reason, I encourage you to take full advantage of qualified retirement plans, such as IRAs and 401(k), 403(b), or other retirement plans that allow you to invest pretax dollars. This includes the Roth IRA, even though you fund it with after-tax dollars.

Income Tax at Withdrawal

No one wants to pay more taxes than they have to, and you aren't legally or morally obligated to do so. That's why many experts are down on variable annuities.

The IRS taxes annuity distributions as ordinary income subject to your individual tax rate, which could be as high as 35 percent.

For fixed annuities, the tax treatment of distributions is comparable to that of other savings products, such as bank CDs or bonds. Part of your payment will be interest and taxable, but most will be return of principal and will not be taxable. (More about this later in the chapter.)

For variable annuities, however, the comparison is to a portfolio of mutual funds, and here the tax treatments differ significantly. The IRS taxes most of the gains in a mutual fund sale (assuming a one-year or longer holding period) at long-term capital gain rates of 15 percent.

There's the problem: Income taxed at 35 percent or 15 percent. Which do you choose? It's not quite that simple, but you see why some folks don't like variable annuities.

Qualified Annuity Taxes

Qualified annuities, those used in an IRS-approved retirement plan, operate under the guidelines and restrictions of the retirement plan.

If you use an annuity as the funding vehicle for an IRA, the rules for IRAs apply to the annuity regarding contributions, withdrawals, and tax treatment.

Pretax Dollar Contributions

If the retirement plan uses pretax dollars (and most do), you can fund an annuity within the plan and reduce your current income tax bill.

Regular fixed annuities are common components of many retirement plans, such as 401(k)s and, in particular, 403(b)s. Variable annuities are not well suited for qualified retirement plans because of their high fees.

What Are the Limits?

All qualified retirement plans have limits to the amount of contributions you can make and how and when distributions occur. If you use an annuity within a qualified retirement plan, you must abide by the plan's rules, even though they would not normally apply to an annuity.

 Careful _____

> It is easy to get confused with multiple retirement accounts, but don't forget that qualified plans require distributions by a certain age—usually by the April after you turn $70^1/_2$. You may face penalties if you miss this date.

Taxed as Ordinary Income

As with distributions from nonqualified annuities, you pay ordinary income taxes on the withdrawals you make from your qualified annuity.

However, because you funded the annuity with pretax dollars, you may pay taxes on every penny you withdraw from a qualified annuity. Taxes on distributions depend on the qualified plan and how it is structured.

Figuring Taxes

When taxes are involved, there are no simple answers, but I'll try to keep this as straightforward as possible. You don't need to know all the nuts and bolts of how this works unless you're curious, but you do need to know what to expect.

Salespeople trying to talk you into some other product will cite taxes as one of the main reasons to avoid annuities. They make the thought of paying ordinary income tax sound obscene.

Annuity salespeople, on the other hand, will list a host of other benefits that show that taxes aren't really that big of a deal.

Here's how taxes on annuities work—you can decide for yourself.

Income vs. Capital Gain

The biggest complaint about variable annuities is that you pay ordinary income tax on distributions and not capital gains tax. When we look at variable annuities in detail, you'll see that they are mutual funds wrapped in an insurance policy.

You pay long-term capital gains tax on profits from a mutual fund held longer than one year. That tax rate is 15 percent at its highest (depending on your income, it could drop to 5 percent).

The highest federal ordinary income tax rate is 35 percent, so it is easy to see why critics think paying the capital gains tax is a better deal. If you add in state and local income taxes, the picture becomes even bleaker.

The Exclusion Ratio

The account balance of a nonqualified fixed annuity consists of the premium and interest earned or investment gains. As you begin withdrawals, the IRS has devised a way to determine how much of each payment to you is taxable.

They use a formula called the exclusion ratio, which is calculated by dividing the total investment in the annuity by the expected return.

 Careful

> Salespeople trying to talk you into another product may harp on the taxes you pay with annuities. The truth is that you pay no more taxes on a fixed annuity payout than you would on any other savings investment. You pay taxes only on the profit.

Investment in the fixed annuity is the premium you paid into the contract; the expected return is the total amount you will receive. That amount depends on which payout option you choose.

When you make that calculation, you get a percentage. You apply that percentage to each payment to get the tax-free portion of the payment.

Figuring Taxes on Fixed Annuities

Let's say that Sally invests $100,000 in a nonqualified fixed annuity and chooses a 15-year certain payout option, which means she will receive monthly payments for 15 years (or her beneficiary will, if she dies before the 15 years is up).

Investment:	$100,000
Monthly payment:	$765
Total return:	$137,700 ($765 × 12 × 15)
Exclusion ratio:	72.6% ($100,000 ÷ $137,700)

Using the exclusion ratio of 72.6 percent, you can calculate that $555.39 of each payment is tax-free ($765 × .726 = $555.39).

If Sally had chosen a single-life payout option, the only change would be in calculating the total return. The IRS provides tables of *life expectancy* to use for the calculation. You use the life expectancy to determine the total return. Based on Sally's age, her life expectancy is 21 years. Here's how the example changes:

Investment: $100,000

Monthly payment: $637

Total return: $160,524 ($637 × 12 × 21)

Exclusion ratio: 62.3% ($100,000 ÷ $160,524)

Using the exclusion ratio of 62.3 percent, you can calculate that $396.82 of each payment is tax-free.

If Sally lives 21 years, this formula works fine. What happens if she lives longer? The IRS, not known for its generosity, will fully tax the entire $637.

Financial Speak

Life expectancy is a term used in the life insurance industry that seems self-explanatory. However, there is a very sophisticated science behind the numbers. Actuaries use complicated mathematical models to arrive at these numbers. They are meant to be accurate not for individuals, but for large groups of people. You can find life expectancy tables online at the IRS website at www.irs.gov/publications/p590/ar02.html#d0e12021.

This illustration uses a single-life payout situation. For joint life or joint/survivor annuities, the IRS uses different tables and multipliers, but the process is much the same.

Other payouts, including cash or installment refunds, also require different calculations.

Figuring Taxes on Variable Annuities

When it comes to calculating taxes on variable annuities, the process is somewhat confusing. Some contracts allow you to take a variable payout, meaning that your monthly check will be more or less, depending on how well your investments perform. We discuss this more in Chapter 11.

Owners of variable annuities can choose to take a fixed payout or a variable payout. You figure the taxes on a fixed payout, as in the fixed annuity example in the previous section, because the insurance company annuitizes the sum just the same.

Some contracts allow you to place a portion of your balance in the fixed account and leave the remainder invested in the variable account. Not all variable annuities permit the same movement; check these details before you buy.

However, if you choose the variable payout, the calculation changes. Because the payments fluctuate with the market, you can't know the expected return, which is part of the equation. In this case, you use the life expectancy figure (21 years, from our previous example) and multiply it by 12 to convert it to months.

You divide the investment in the variable annuity by this number.

For example:

Sally invested $100,000 in a variable annuity and chose variable payouts. Her life expectancy is 21 years. What portion of each monthly payout would be tax-free?

Investment: $100,000

Life expectancy: 21 years

(21 × 12 = 252 months)   ($100,000 ÷ 252 = $396.82)

This calculation tells her that each month, $396.82 of her payment is tax-free and the rest must be declared.

Figuring Taxes on Withdrawals

Withdrawals present a different problem. By their definition, you may or may not make them, and they may vary in size from one to the next. As we learned earlier, systematic withdrawals have some major benefits over annuitization.

However, one of the drawbacks is the way the IRS treats them for tax purposes. There are different rules for annuities purchased before 1982, but I'm assuming those don't apply to you.

In a rare display of simplicity, the IRS says if you make withdrawals from an annuity, what comes out first are the earnings.

For example, suppose you bought a $100,000 annuity, and it grew to $125,000. When you begin making withdrawals, the IRS considers the first $25,000 you take out as 100 percent earnings and taxable.

As you can see, this is not nearly as attractive as spreading the taxable income over a period of years like annuitization does.

 Consider This _____

> Withdrawals offer a way to time not only your income, but also your tax liability. You may want to make initial withdrawals during periods when other income is low, to offset the taxes you pay on the earnings in those early withdrawals.

At the risk of repeating myself, any withdrawal before age 59$\frac{1}{2}$ will draw a 10-percent penalty from the IRS.

Don't Sweat Tax Calculations

You don't have to worry about doing all of these calculations yourself. The salesperson will be able to show you the tax consequences of any payout option you choose.

However, now you have a general understanding of how taxation works and can make better decisions about payout options. You also have a clearer picture of the true tax reality.

Taxes and Beneficiaries

One of the other major complaints about annuities is that they pass to beneficiaries (not spouses) as taxable events in most cases.

This means the annuity passes to the beneficiary with a tax bill right off the bat, as in the case of a lump-sum distribution, or one comes at the end of the year, in the case of periodic payments.

How this affects beneficiaries depends on which phase the annuity is in and which payout option the owner selected.

No Step-Up

Annuity opponents point out that when a mutual fund portfolio passes to a beneficiary, the IRS considers its value at that date the starting point for taxes.

In other words, if Uncle Harry leaves you his $100,000 in mutual funds with a built-in gain of $25,000 on October 1, that becomes your basis, for tax purposes. You don't owe any taxes on the $100,000 or the $25,000 gain; you pay only if the value of the portfolio increases above $100,000.

The industry calls this a step-up in value. However, if Aunt Sally leaves you a $100,000 annuity that has a current value of $150,000, you're on the hook for taxes on the $50,000 in profits.

Taxes After Annuitization

If the owner dies after annuitization has begun, the beneficiary generally continues to receive the payout option in progress. The taxes depend on what that option is and how much remains on the annuity's payout.

If the payout is a single life with no refund options selected, payments end at death and there is no beneficiary.

The general rules that govern annuity taxation pass on to the beneficiaries.

Taxes Before Annuitization

If the owner dies before annuitization has begun, usually the beneficiary must take the money in some form, either in a lump sum within 5 years or accept the terms of the annuity payout and begin taking payments within one year. As an example, if the owner set the annuity up as a 15-year payout, the beneficiary could choose this option within one year of the owner's death.

In each case, there is no step-up in basis for tax purposes. The beneficiary must deal with the full tax consequences.

The exception to this is that a surviving spouse may continue the contract as the new owner if named as the beneficiary of the annuity, with no tax consequences.

Early Withdrawal

Although noted elsewhere, it bears repeating: The IRS will sock you with a 10-percent penalty for taking money out of your annuity before age $59^1/_2$. This is on top of any other fees the insurance company might charge.

There are some exceptions, such as disability or death, but, for the most part, don't even think about pulling out money except in a real emergency (new golf clubs are not an emergency).

1035 Exchanges

While we are on the subject of taxes, now is a good time to introduce the Section 1035 Exchanges. This refers to a section of the IRS code that permits tax-free exchanges of like-kind contracts. For annuity owners, it is a way to get out of a bad contract or into a better one without paying taxes on any profits.

Tax-Free Exchanges

The IRS allows the following exchanges:

- A contract of life insurance for an annuity contract
- An annuity contract for another annuity

Why would you want to get out of an annuity contract? Maybe you became concerned about the financial stability of the life insurance company that wrote the contract (a major service might have lowered its rating).

Your personal financial needs might have changed, and another annuity might offer features that fit your circumstances. Perhaps your nephew is just starting out in the life insurance business, and you would like to help him get started.

Whatever the reason, 1035 Exchanges can move you from one contract to another with no tax liability. However, remember the phrase "like kind." You can exchange contracts of essentially the same kind for others of the same kind.

Watch Out for Traps

Watch out for two cautions when executing 1035 Exchanges.

First, you should let the life insurance companies handle the funds directly during the exchange. The companies will be glad to do this, and it should be the normal way the process works.

The IRS doctrine of "constructive receipt" says if you have access to the funds, it can tax them. So, don't surrender your old contract and buy a new one, and then try to claim it was a 1035 Exchange—that won't fly with the IRS.

The second trap is in the form of hungry salespeople who will try to flip you out of one contract and into another so they can earn a commission.

 **Careful** _____

There may be a good reason to exchange one annuity contract for another, but be sure you look at both contracts carefully. Are you paying fees to get out of one only to get a bonus interest rate in the other? Does that make any sense?

Be aware that you may pay a surrender fee to get out of your old contract, and that loss could offset any gain the salesperson is trying to sell.

We discuss fees in greater detail in Chapter 10, but it may not make much sense to drop one contract and pay a surrender fee just to pick up a new contract.

The Least You Need to Know

- The IRS taxes profits from annuities as ordinary income
- Part of an annuity payment is return of principal, and part is profit.
- The exclusion ratio is a calculation to figure how much of an annuity payment is tax-free.
- Beneficiaries must pay taxes on the accumulated earnings in an annuity contract. There is no step-up in basis.

Chapter 6

Fixed Annuities

In This Chapter

- Fixed annuities explained
- What they pay
- Types of fixed annuities
- Fixed annuity fees and risks

Fixed annuities are the workhorses of the annuity family. The number of fixed annuities exceeds all other types simply because these have been around the longest and are found in many qualified retirement plans.

Fixed annuities are easy to understand and offer all the benefits that buyers are looking for: security, a decent return for a savings instrument, and tax-deferred growth.

Unlike their flashy cousins, variable annuities, fixed annuities seldom keep anyone up at night with worry. In fact, life insurance companies design them so you can get a good night's sleep knowing your money is safe.

Getting a Fix on Annuities

A fixed annuity is a contract between you and a life insurance company. Like most contracts, it spells out terms and conditions that both parties must meet and penalties if one party fails to meet the conditions, and it is binding. This means that there is legal authority behind the contract.

If that sounds intimidating, don't worry—it's not as bad as it sounds. Many of the "legal" requirements are on the insurance company and not the consumer, and the others are there to earn the annuity its tax-deferred status.

It's Your Money

The fixed annuity offers a feature unique in the financial services industry: a guaranteed income for life.

In its simplest form, you can reduce the fixed annuity to the following statement: *In exchange for your premium, the insurance company agrees to pay you a stated interest; to guarantee the return of your principal, at least; to provide tax-deferred growth; and to guarantee you an income for life, if you pick that payout option.*

This simplicity makes fixed annuities an easy choice for many people looking for an investment vehicle to augment their retirement plan.

Fixed annuities are widely used in retirement plans because they offer an attractive and secure fixed-income component. Their predictable returns and safety are nice counters to the vagrancies of the stock market.

Tax-Sheltered Annuities

Retirement plans for governmental, nonprofit, or charity organizations, known as 403(b)plans, use tax-sheltered annuities as their main funding vehicle.

You can buy these inside a qualified 403(b) retirement plan—and because they are part of a qualified retirement plan, there are rules concerning contributions and distributions that differ from nonqualified annuities.

Other retirement plans, such as IRAs and 401(k) plans, use regular annuities as funding vehicles. When used inside a qualified plan, those rules govern contributions and distributions.

Tax-Deferred Earnings

Earnings grow tax-deferred in a nonqualified fixed annuity, which makes them an attractive supplement for funding retirements without the restrictions placed on qualified plans.

In addition, there is no reasonable limit, except as placed by the insurance company, on how much you can invest in annuities.

Understanding What They Pay

Many different types of fixed annuities exist, as we discuss later in the chapter. The life insurance companies are very creative when it comes to inventing new annuity products and marketing them.

Guaranteed Rate

For basic fixed annuities, the contract calls for a guaranteed interest rate for a certain period. This guarantee period can range from 1 to 10 years. During this time, the interest rate can't change. A surrender charge period usually exceeds the rate guarantee period. This charge is a disincentive to surrender (cash in) the annuity.

At the end of the guarantee period, you have the option either to take advantage of another rate guarantee period or to let the annuity rate float with market rates, called the renewal rate. If you choose another rate guarantee period, you start a new surrender charges period.

Bonus Rates

Some annuities offer a much higher rate the first year as an incentive to buy the product. The next year, the rate drops back to a reasonable market level.

Bonus rates most often work for single-premium deferred annuities, in which you are depositing a lump sum.

Many providers offer higher rates for larger single-premium deferred annuities because the maintenance costs on such accounts are lower.

Single or Flexible Premium

You can buy fixed annuities with either a single premium or a flexible premium. The single-premium annuity requires a lump-sum payment up front and accepts no future payments. The flexible premium does allow you to make future payments.

The benefit of the single premium is that your money goes to work faster. Many of the bonus-rate annuities require a single premium. Minimum premiums tend to be no lower than $5,000. For very large premiums, the life insurance companies may pay higher rates. Annuities used in qualified plans have different contribution requirements.

The advantage of the flexible premium is that you can open them with a smaller balance and periodically add to the annuity. Some companies will set up an automatic debit from your bank account.

The insurance company may charge you a fee to use flexible premiums due to increased maintenance costs on the account.

Surrender Charges

Fixed annuities have fees called a "back-end load." This means you pay no sales fees up front when you buy the annuity. However, if you cash in the annuity during the period when surrender fees are in effect, the insurance company will charge your account the prevailing fee.

Here's how that works. An annuity might have surrender charges that last seven years, but the rate guarantee lasts only three years. This means that at the end of three years, you are at the mercy of the life insurance company to pay a competitive rate for the remaining years of the surrender charges. For example:

Years	Rate Guarantee	Surrender Charges
1	4%	7%
2	4%	6%
3	4%	5%
4	—	4%
5	—	3%
6	—	2%
7	—	1%

The purpose of the surrender charge is to discourage you from taking your money out of the account. It also protects an insurance company (like they really need protecting) from liquidity crunches.

Most companies will let you lock in another rate guarantee period when the first runs out, but the surrender charge clock restarts.

Your other choice is to see if the company is paying a competitive interest rate without the guarantee in place. If not, you can wait until the surrender charges expire and surrender the annuity for cash.

Careful

Surrender charges are an acceptable part of fixed annuities; however, watch out when they go overboard. For example, if a salesperson offers you an annuity with a 1-year rate guarantee and a 10-year surrender charge period, you should ask why.

If you are in fixed deferred annuities for the long term (and that's the only way you should be), surrender charges usually don't come into play.

You can find annuities that avoid the problem of the interest rate guarantee ending before the surrender charges, if that's a concern. Many people just keep signing up for another guarantee period to lock in a competitive rate and don't worry about the surrender charges.

Other Features

All fixed annuity contracts contain similar language and provisions concerning some basic contract features. These features usually give you some rights or define what will happen in certain circumstances.

Free Withdrawals

Most annuities allow you to withdraw a certain amount each year without paying any fees, although the IRS will still want its 10 percent if you are under age 59$^{1}/_{2}$.

How much you can withdraw varies with each company, but up to 10 percent of the account value is typical. Even though you can do it, it's not a good idea. You are putting money in an annuity so it can earn interest; taking some out defeats the purpose.

Loans

Some contracts allow you to borrow money from your account, although you should be aware that a loan is the same as a distribution for tax purposes, so you will owe taxes on the amount. Also, the IRS will want its 10 percent if you are under 59$^{1}/_{2}$.

Borrowing from your annuity should be a last resort. Remember, the idea is for your money to grow so you can enjoy retirement.

 Consider This

> Borrowing money from your annuity (or any retirement account, for that matter) is generally a bad idea. The benefit of tax-deferred growth is to let your money keep compounding as long as possible. Look for other sources of cash to fund college, a new house, a car, and so forth.

Free Look

All annuity contracts (including equity-indexed and variable annuities) have a free-look clause. This clause gives purchasers the opportunity to change their minds.

Regulators recognize that annuities can seem confusing when presented by less than ethical salespeople, and you could suffer buyer's remorse. The free-look period gives you the chance to look over the contract and get expert advice, if necessary.

If you change your mind during the free-look period, the company must return your money. Free-look periods range from 10 to 30 days.

Issue Ages

Most contracts for deferred annuities allow issue ages up to 90 or higher, although some companies may put conditions on ages above 76. Few age restrictions affect immediate annuities.

Maturity Date

Annuity contracts specify a maturity date—in many cases, this is age 85 or 90. It could also be 10 years from the contract anniversary, if that were later than age 90 of the owner.

The life insurance company automatically annuitizes the contract on this date—at least, that's the theory. In fact, the contract holder often changes it.

Fixed Deferred Annuities

Thanks to a competitive market, many different types of fixed annuities exist. This means there is a good chance you will find one that meets your particular needs.

All of the major insurance companies put their own spin on product types for competitive purposes. I describe the major types of fixed annuities, but be aware that you will find products on the market with names that don't sound like any of these.

It's Your Money

Insurance companies sell annuities under a variety of names, some of which may sound like the types listed here, but many will not. However, a reading of the contract will quickly identify the type of annuity and what features it offers.

They all will work approximately the same, and when you have a basic understanding of these types, it isn't hard to figure out some new configuration.

CD-Type Deferred Annuity

Annuities compete directly with bank certificates of deposit for savings dollars. One of the ways insurance companies have reacted to this competition is to create an annuity that looks and acts like a bank CD.

The CD-type or certificate annuity has a rate guarantee period that matches the surrender charge period. In other words, when the interest rate guarantee period ends, so do the surrender charges. This means that at the end of this period, you can surrender the annuity without paying any charges. You also have the option of renewing the certificate annuity for another guaranteed period. It's no accident that bank CDs work the same way.

This product prevents you from being locked into an annuity that is paying a noncompetitive interest rate because surrender charges would take too big of a chunk of your capital.

Market Value Adjusted Annuity

Market value adjusted (MVA) annuities tie the account value to market interest rates, so the value of your account is adjusted to reflect higher or lower prevailing interest rates.

You should earn a higher interest rate for an MVA annuity because there is some risk that your account value will fall based on market interest rates. Of course, it also could rise. In most cases, there is a floor under the asset value of your account. The downside will never eat into your principal, though, so what's at risk is your earnings.

These annuities have an upside, too, because your account value may rise in the right interest-rate environment.

Bonus Rate Annuity

Bonus rate annuities offer a higher interest rate the first year and then a reduced rate the reminder of the guarantee period.

Insurance companies offer these simply to get you to buy, and there is nothing wrong with that. However, be careful that there is not a hook in that piece of bait.

The hook might be in the form of a lower interest rate after the bonus period expires or an exceptionally long surrender charge period.

Look closely at all the factors before swallowing the bait. It might be a great deal, but you may also wish you hadn't swallowed.

Bailout Annuity

A bailout annuity lets you cash in without surrender charges if the renewal rate falls below a level set forth in the contract.

Once the guaranteed interest rate period is up, the insurance company sets a renewal rate. If that rate is below the bailout rate stated in the contract, you have the right to liquidate your annuity without surrender charges. This feature protects you from the insurance company setting low renewal rates in a rising interest rate market.

Interest-Indexed Deferred Annuity

Many annuities now use an interest rate indexing method to set the renewal rate after the initial guarantee rate expires. The insurance companies use a known index, such as 10-year Treasury notes.

Careful _____

> Certain annuities, both indexed and market value adjusted, offer no guaranteed protection of principal. These annuities are registered securities and fall under the variable annuity category.

This prevents the life insurance company from taking advantage of annuity owners once the guarantee rate expires. How the renewal rate is calculated should be in the contract. This will give you an idea of what to expect when the guaranteed interest rate expires.

Some contracts offer fully indexed renewal rates, while others offer only partially indexed renewal rates. The partially indexed contract places a cap on the rate the insurer guarantees at renewal.

Split-Funded Annuity

A split-funded annuity is really not a single annuity, but a combination of two annuities to provide immediate income and restore the original principal. It's the basic "having your cake and eating it, too."

Here's how it works: You split your principal and buy a deferred annuity with one part and an immediate annuity with the other part. The idea is that the immediate (period certain) annuity liquidates itself concurrent with the deferred annuity, earning back enough to replenish all of the original capital.

The calculation to figure this is fairly complicated, so an annuity salesperson will need to tell you what you can expect.

I compare the split-funded annuity to a CD because you receive income for a period and your principal remains intact.

This example shows how a split-funded annuity works. At the end of eight years, you have received nearly $34,000 in income, most of which is not taxable, and you still have your original $100,000 starting principal.

> $30,000* Immediate annuity 8-year period certain at 4.3% monthly income of $345 results in total income of $33,900*.

> $70,000* Deferred annuity 8-year guaranteed interest rate at 4.35% grows tax-deferred restores principle of $100,000.

> *Numbers are rounded off and are approximate and for illustration only.

As you can see, the split-funded annuity can be a powerful tool if you don't need the income from your full principal amount. As interest rates change, you can adjust the amounts and periods according to your needs. Another benefit is that you can withdraw money from the deferred annuity in the event of certain emergencies (disability or nursing home admission, for example).

Risks with Fixed Annuities

Security is the No. 1 reason people buy fixed annuities. They want to sleep well at night, and annuities let them do just that.

However, that's not to say they are risk-free. Anytime you have a financial product that is sensitive to interest rates and is a long-term investment, there are risks involved.

It's Your Money

Fixed annuities offer little market protection against interest rate increases and inflation. That's why you should consider keeping a portion of your retirement portfolio in the market based on your risk tolerance and financial goals.

Interest Rate Risk

One of the biggest risks of fixed annuities is the danger of locking in a low interest rate and having rates move higher.

Several of the products described in this chapter attempt to mitigate this risk, but annuities remain a nonliquid investment without the means to move assets to more interest-advantaged areas quickly. Even those products that attempt to react to the market may adjust only once a year.

Most annuity buyers are willing to give up some market advantage for the security they get. However, in very low-interest markets, annuities and other savings instruments suffer nearly flat returns when you factor in inflation and taxes that you will pay eventually.

Inflation Risk

The inflation rate has been relatively low for a number of years, but even a small rate can cut into your savings every year. Inflation is an invisible tax we all pay, but people on fixed incomes suffer the most. There is no way for regular fixed annuities to combat inflation effectively. You need another tool in your portfolio to offset inflation.

The Least You Need to Know

- Fixed annuities are the simplest and most common types of annuities.
- Fixed annuities pay a guaranteed interest rate for a period and then a renewal rate, which could be lower.
- Several different types of fixed annuities exist, to fit a variety of financial needs.
- Surrender charges are fees you must pay if you cash in your annuity before a certain period expires.

Chapter 7

Equity-Indexed Annuities

In This Chapter

- Components of equity-indexed annuities
- Various indexing methods
- Risks and potential rewards

Equity-indexed annuities seem to have it all: guaranteed minimum contract value, the opportunity to participate in long-term growth of the stock market, no loss of accumulated earnings (no downside), and no investment decisions to make. So, what's not to like?

Well, there's the possibility of flat or negative real returns when inflation is considered, along with the fact that you may not know what your equity-indexed annuity is worth until the end of a lengthy period with some varieties. However, the chance to earn near-market returns with virtually no downside has made these annuities very popular.

People buy fixed annuities for their low risk and predictability; however, equity-indexed annuities fill another financial need. With low rates on savings for several years, products that offer the opportunity to earn near–stock market returns but with limited risk attract attention.

The equity-indexed annuity ties your potential earnings to the overall movement of a key market index, while protecting the integrity of most of your capital. Any earnings stay in the account and are not at risk by a subsequent market downturn. Equity-indexed annuities are very popular with investors who are looking for something beyond a savings instrument but who are not quite ready for full exposure to the stock market.

A Hybrid Annuity

The equity-indexed annuity is a fixed annuity with a guaranteed minimum contract value, a guaranteed minimum interest rate (in most cases), and the opportunity to earn more interest based on the performance of a key market index. It features all the characteristics of regular deferred annuities:

- **Death benefit**—The usual death benefits are available during the accumulation and distribution phases.
- **Tax deferral**—Your earnings grow tax-deferred while they remain in the account, and you pay taxes only when you begin withdrawals.
- **Distribution**—The usual payout options are available, including annuitizing the account.

The index-linked interest distinguishes the equity-indexed annuity from a regular fixed annuity. A formula measures the performance of the index and converts it into a percentage, which another formula applies to your account balance.

For example, if you bought an equity-indexed annuity linked to the S&P 500 Index for $100,000, and at the end of a five-year term, the S&P had risen 20 percent, the life insurance company would credit your account with $20,000. It's much more complicated than that, but you get the general idea.

 Consider This _____

> The first equity-indexed annuity made its debut in 1995, copying similar products in England. So it is also the newest of the three types of annuities (fixed, equity-indexed, and variable) covered in this book.

Major Components

Equity-indexed annuities consist of several key components. Understanding these components is a big step toward getting a grip on how equity-indexed annuities work. Like other products, they come in many forms, so what is true for one may not be true for the next. Read all contracts carefully so you'll understand what you're buying. The major pieces are the contract value and guaranteed interest rates, the indexes, averaging, the participation rate, the cap rate, the indexing method, the fees, and the interest calculation. An equity-indexed annuity is a combination of all of these factors.

Contract Value and Minimum Interest Rates

Although equity-indexed annuities start out as fixed annuities, they take on some major changes that you should note. The biggest change is in guarantees of contract value and interest rates.

I must say directly that it is possible, although not likely, to lose money with some equity-indexed annuities. This is part of the price you pay for potentially higher returns. I'll explain how you can lose money later in the chapter.

Unlike regular fixed annuities, many equity-indexed annuities do not guarantee 100 percent return of your premium. A common guarantee is a minimum contract value of 90 percent of the premium plus the guaranteed interest. You can find some equity-indexed annuities that guarantee 100 percent return of your premium, but they are in the minority and there is usually a compromise elsewhere in the contract.

As with fixed annuities, most equity-indexed annuities pay a minimum guaranteed interest rate for the term of the annuity, or at least part of the term. The most frequent rate is 3 percent. Most contracts have a fixed account within the annuity where cash earns the guaranteed interest rate.

The contract will state when you can transfer money to the equity-linked portion of the account. Some annuities have more than one index, and some may include a bond index.

Combined with the 90 percent guarantee (lower in some contracts, higher in others), the 3 percent minimum rate hardly makes an attractive package. However, the equity-indexed annuity investor is more interested in the upside from the other part of the product than a safe place to put her money.

 Careful

> If you need or expect a certain return for your financial plan to work, equity-indexed annuities may not be the right vehicle for you. Consider a fixed annuity instead.

The Indexes

The market indexes that are used to calculate interest increases in equity-indexed annuities are measurements of specific segments of the stock market. They reflect how these different segments react to economic and other factors.

An index is a mathematical device for monitoring change, especially for a large group of variable numbers such as stock prices. Without going into a very complicated math lesson, an index establishes a base and then measures the movement of the group against the base.

Here is a listing and brief description of the most widely used indexes:

S&P 500 Index. This is the most widely used and accepted index of market behavior in the financial world. It has been around in some form for more than 50 years, and it currently measures the movement of 500 market-leading stocks.

Dow Jones Industrial Average. This index measures 30 of the largest, most prestigious companies on the market.

Nasdaq 100. This index includes the largest 100 domestic and foreign nonfinancial companies listed on the Nasdaq, based on *market capitalization*. It tends to list younger, more entrepreneurial companies.

Russell 2000 Index. The Frank Russell Company, now a part of Northwestern Mutual, developed the Russell 2000 Index of 2,000 smaller companies. It has numerous other indexes that measure other market segments.

$ **Financial Speak**

Market capitalization is a term used to describe a company's size relative to its market price. You compute the market cap by multiplying the stock's price by the number of outstanding shares. For example, if a company's stock is selling for $65 per share and there are 120 million shares outstanding, the market cap is $7.8 billion.

Averaging

The life insurance company calculates the interest on an equity-indexed annuity based on the change in the value of the linked index. The greater that change is, the more interest you earn. The starting value is usually the day you buy the annuity.

This raises an obvious question: How do you avoid buying on the day the index is at its highest or at a high point? If you buy at this point, you may limit your interest when the term expires.

Some equity-indexed annuities (certainly not all) use an averaging method to avoid this problem. They use an average—usually a month—value as the starting point and do the same thing when the contract matures. Although this may avoid buying high and selling low, it also may lower the amount you could potentially receive.

Participation Rate

The participation rate of a particular equity-indexed annuity is an important piece of information if you are comparing one annuity to another. The participation rate determines how much of the increase in the index's value the contract applies to your account. For example, if an equity-indexed annuity's participation rate is 80 percent and the calculated change in the linked index is 18 percent, your account receives only 14.4 percent interest. (18 percent × 80 percent = 14.4 percent)

The insurance company sets the participation rate at the time of purchase and guarantees it anywhere from a year to the entire term of the contract. However, some contracts permit participation rates to change during the term. Read the contract carefully so you are not unpleasantly surprised by a lower participation rate.

 Careful

> Read the contract carefully, and ask questions if something isn't clear. Some life insurance companies write contracts with participation rates that change during the life of the contract. Buyer, beware.

As we'll see later in this chapter, the participation rate combined with the indexing method tells the true picture of what the equity-indexed annuity may yield.

Cap Rate

Some equity-indexed annuities have a cap rate on the interest they will pay, no matter what. For example, the contract may say it will not pay more than 12 percent interest; so no matter what the linked index does, you can't earn more than 12 percent.

Indexing Method

The method used to calculate the change in the index is one of the most important features of an equity-indexed annuity. This calculation determines how much, if any, interest the insurance company credits to your account and when that occurs.

Three major methods are used: annual reset or ratchet, high water mark, and point-to-point. Which of the three indexing methods is the best? Each has some advantages and disadvantages, but you need to evaluate them in the context of all the other components. For example, one might offer a higher rate, but it might also carry a lower participation rate or higher margin/spread/fee.

The following sections describe each major method and also point out the advantages and disadvantages of each.

Annual Reset or Ratchet

This method looks at the index value at the end of one year after you bought the contract and applies the increase, if any. Every following contract anniversary, the insurance company looks at the index.

Two things happen at the end of each contract year: The contract establishes a new value for the index for the next year, and your account earnings are locked in so any future declines in the index won't affect your account. For example:

End of Year	Index	Percent Increase	Account
0	100	—	$100
1	110	10%	$110
2	105	0%	$110
3	106	1%	$111
4	111	5%	$116
5	108	0%	$116

This chart illustrates that even when the index lost ground in two years out of five, the account did not lose accumulated earnings.

Advantages: The annual reset or ratchet method of indexing is the most desirable on the surface because it locks in gains each year. This means you won't be hurt if third year of a five-year contract is terrible because the contract has locked in the gains of the first two years.

Disadvantages: This form of indexing is so attractive that the insurance companies build in some conditions to slow down the account growth. Contracts with an annual reset or ratchet method of indexing are more likely to have lower participation rates, higher margin/spread/asset fees, or interest caps than other indexing methods.

Conclusion: If you can find an equity-indexed annuity without too many constraints that uses this method of indexing, it may be your best choice.

High Water Mark

The high water mark method of indexing looks at points during the term of the contract and compares them to the starting point (the day you bought the annuity). It uses the highest of these to compute the increase, if any.

The usual dates for checking are on the annual anniversaries of the contract because equity-indexed annuities tend to run five years and longer terms. For example, a five-year contract would have checks at the end of each year, including the end date. Of those five checks, the contract would use the highest index value to compute the interest. If the index was at its highest on the three-year check, that number would be used to compute your interest. For example:

First of Year	Index
0	100
1	110
2	105
3	106
4	111
5	108

This chart shows a five-year look at the index on the anniversary of the purchase. The highest mark was on the fourth year at 111, which translates into an 11.1 percent increase for the term of the contract. The life insurance company would credit a $100,000 account with $11,100 interest for the period. Of course, there would be other fees and considerations, so this chart is just to illustrate the indexing method and is not an actual representation of what might end up in your pocket.

Advantages: This method looks at the index on specific contract anniversary dates and picks the highest one. You have a good chance that the number will be high on one of the dates.

Disadvantages: The insurance company does not credit interest to your account until the end of the term, so you don't know what the contract is worth until then. If you surrender the contract early, you may not receive any index-linked interest. Some contracts allow crediting of partial interest in early surrender situations. Insurance companies may use limiting factors, such as lower participation rates or higher margin/spread/asset fees, with this indexing method.

Conclusion: The high water mark method of indexing works best if the index hits its high early in the term and then falls toward the end. However, it is not a bad method even in normal markets, as long as the contract doesn't contain too many limiting factors.

Point-to-Point

The point-to-point indexing method is the simplest to understand, but it carries the most risk.

With this indexing method, you compare the value of the index on the day you purchased the annuity to the value of the index on the final day of the contract's term, to arrive at a difference. The insurance company converts this difference into a percentage and applies it to your account.

Advantages: The point-to-point method of indexing is simplicity in itself: What was the value of the index on the day you bought the contract, and what was the value of the index on the day the term expired? The difference is the interest applied to your account. This method of indexing often draws the highest participation rate.

Disadvantages: The contract does not credit interest until the end of the term. If you surrender the contract early, you may lose any index-linked interest. Because the annuity calculates interest on two dates—the beginning and ending of the contract term—you run the risk of catching the index wrong on those two days. It may be high on the purchase day and may continue to gain the life of the contract, only to fall dramatically the day you sell, wiping out any gains.

Conclusion: This indexing method carries more risk than the others, but it holds out more potential gain. Participation rates are typically higher, and if the market is moving forward, you stand to make substantial gains.

Equity-Indexed Annuity Fees

These are an ugly deduction that insurance companies may use with or instead of the participation rate to reduce how much interest you earn. It goes by different names, margin, spread, asset, or administration fee, but it means the same thing: less money for you.

The insurance company sets the fee at, for example, 3.5 percent. The company then reduces the computed increase in the linked index by that much. For example, if the index rose 11 percent, the company would credit your account with 7.5 percent increase. (11 percent − 3.5 percent = 7.5 percent)

In addition to these types of fees, many equity-indexed annuities carry surrender charges, which often last the term of the contract.

It's Your Money

Surrender charges for equity-indexed annuities may run the full term of the contract. The insurance companies really discourage you (and I do, too) from pulling out money early.

You will also pay a penalty to the IRS if you withdraw money before age $59^{1/2}$ from the annuity. When you add these fees and penalties to the fact that early surrender may also mean the loss of all or part of any index-linked interest, you realize that these are truly long-term commitments.

Equity-Indexed Annuity Risks

Anytime you are tying an investment to the performance of the stock market, risks are involved in the transaction. Although the equity-indexed annuity is not as risky as the variable annuity, it carries its own set of dangers.

Most equity-indexed annuities are not registered securities and do not come under the scrutiny of the Securities and Exchange Commission or the National Association of Securities Dealers.

You Can Lose Money

As you learned with fixed annuities, the worst that can happen is that you get your premium back (or your heirs do). That's not the case with equity-indexed annuities.

If the linked index does not rise during the term of the contract, or rises and falls at the wrong time, you may not receive any interest beyond the guaranteed 3 percent and whatever the premium guarantee was (in many cases, no more than 90 percent).

If you surrender the contract early, you may not receive any index-linked interest, and you will have to pay surrender charges.

Interest Rate Risk

This is the risk of investing in an equity-indexed annuity that may not pay off versus investing in a fixed annuity with a guaranteed interest rate.

You run the risk of not receiving any interest when you could lock in a certain interest rate. This is part of the risk-reward component of investing. You must be willing to chance earning no interest and even losing money for the potential of making a much higher return.

Inflation Risk

Normally, the stock market is a good inflation hedge, but not always. Periods of high inflation can send the market down, and that could mean little or no index-linked interest.

You could find yourself in the worst possible situation: Your index is dropping and inflation is rising.

The Least You Should Know

- The equity-indexed annuity is a way to participate in the overall growth of a specific segment of the stock market.
- The participation rate, which determines how much of the increase in the index's value the contract applies to your account, is a major determinant of the contract's return.
- The indexing method is how the interest is calculated and is the most important part on the contract.
- It is possible to make a substantial return with an equity-indexed annuity, but you can also lose money.

Variable Annuities

In This Chapter

- History of variable annuities
- Variable annuity components
- Variable annuities in your financial plan

If you were to walk into a room full of financial professionals and shout "variable annuities," it wouldn't be long before arguments would be breaking out all around you.

One group of professionals would argue that variable annuities are the biggest rip-off in town, while another group would argue that variable annuities are the greatest thing since crunchy peanut butter.

Not too many products on the financial scene stir emotions as much or as quickly as variable annuities. In my hypothetical setting, there would be a third group of financial professionals not arguing with anyone. They would be the group to listen to about variable annuities.

They would say that variable annuities may be right for some investors, but not for all, and not all variable annuities are right for anyone. As with any financial product, knowledgeable investors can determine whether variable annuities work for them and then can choose the annuity that makes the most sense.

The best way for you to decide whether variable annuities work for you is to understand the product—its benefits and limitations.

Variable Annuity History

Despite all the recent attention, variable annuities have been around in some form for a number of years. A number of changes in tax laws and a tightening of regulations on what products life insurance companies can include in variable annuities have refined the product to what we know today.

However, major changes in the retirement market are the real force behind the growth of variable annuities. The whole retirement mentality has shifted from reliance on the employer to reliance on the individual. Retirement plans such as 401(k)s and IRAs define contributions but not ultimate benefits.

In the last half of the 1990s, interest rates were low and the stock market experienced an unprecedented boom. People wanted part of their retirement portfolio invested in equities, and variable annuities filled that need for some.

Sales of variable annuities were a mere $3.5 billion in 1990, but they soared to $63 billion in 1999 and were an astounding $985 billion by 2001. A number of factors drove the sales, including these:

- An aging baby boomer generation (people born between 1946 and 1964) looking for ways to add to their retirement nest egg
- Low interest rates on fixed annuities and other savings products
- Aggressive salespeople eager to capture lucrative commissions

All of these factors contributed to making variable annuities one of the hottest products on the market.

Aging Boomers

As the baby boomer generation approaches retirement, more are beginning to realize that their lifestyle of immediate gratification has not left much for a retirement fund.

Traditional savings instruments with low interest aren't very attractive when compared to the gains available in the stock market. Yet, many don't want to completely let go of all the security they may be used to in regular annuities.

Variable annuities fill this void by promising potential market rate gains, while providing some protection. The worst that can happen is that your heirs get most of your premium back.

Low Interest on Savings

Interest rates on savings instruments have been low for a number of years. When you factor in inflation and taxes, returns are flat to negative—not the recommended way to build a retirement fund.

The stock market has historically returned 10 to 12 percent over the past 75 plus years. Certainly, not all stocks or mutual funds have hit this mark; however, if you're looking for the potential for significant gains, it's in the market, not savings instruments.

Aggressive Salespeople

You cannot underestimate the importance of marketing and sales in the growth of variable annuities. If you "follow the money," it's easy to see why.

Commissions on variable annuity sales are very high, which means they will be at the top of many salespeople's list when it's time to visit a client.

Variable annuities are registered securities, and the people who sell them are licensed. This is not a problem because most life insurance people also sell other registered products, and other financial professionals sell variable annuities.

Taking Them Apart

It is common to hear variable annuities called mutual funds wrapped in a life insurance policy. While this is correct, it doesn't go far enough and greatly oversimplifies the product.

A variable annuity has three main components,
which we will look at in more detail: the general
account, which is very similar to a fixed annuity;
the separate account, which houses the variable
investments; and the death benefit (life insurance).

The General Account

The general account holds the fixed portion of
your money in a variable annuity. Most variable
annuities offer a guaranteed interest rate at one or
more periods—one, three, five years, or more, for
example. The life insurance company guarantees
your principal like a regular fixed annuity.

You can move money back and forth between this
account and the separate account where the variable investments reside. However, there may be
a charge if you move money before the interest
guarantee period expires.

It's Your Money

Your variable annuity investment is split
between the general account and the separate account. The life insurance company
invests money held in the general account
and assumes the risk. Money in the separate account goes to subaccounts outside
the insurance company. The annuity owner
assumes the investment risk for this money.

The Separate Account

The separate account is just that: separate from the insurance company's general account. You fund investment options through this account—in other words, the variable part of the variable annuity.

The insurance company does not commingle its funds with the separate account, and the company does not insure this account, except through the death benefit. The account would be safe if creditors seized the assets of the life insurance company.

When the annuity owner directs money to the variable portion of the annuity, it flows through this account to subaccounts, which I discuss in detail in Chapter 9.

The Death Benefit

The traditional death benefit says that your beneficiary will receive the greater of the account value or your premium (less withdrawals) if you die before payments begin. This is how you "break even" no matter how badly the market treats you (of course, dying is a tough price to pay).

I discussed the optional death benefits in Chapter 4, but because of their unique relationship to variable annuities, it is worth briefly revisiting the subject.

The traditional death benefit provides your beneficiary with either your account value, minus withdrawals, or your invested premium, whichever is greater. This is fine for just getting back to even, but if you want to pass on something more to your heirs, the optional death benefits may be the ticket.

Careful

> Optional death benefits cost money. Be sure they add the value you really need before paying for a benefit that may never be used. Term life insurance could accomplish the same goal at a lower cost.

In addition to those discussed in Chapter 4, variable annuity providers offer variations that allow you to lock in investment gains. So even if your investments sour, those gains—or some part of them—are locked into the death benefit. You can't touch them, but your heirs will remember your foresight.

However, these options come with a price tag. Be sure you understand the costs involved and other limitations—some options may have an age limit.

Do *Variable* and *Annuity* Go Together?

Variable annuities seem to fly in the face of two of the reasons people buy annuities: security and predictability.

Sure, the death benefit may return most of your premium to a beneficiary, even if you make lousy investment choices, but that's not unique. Death benefit options can increase their take, but you're still talking about making someone else wealthy.

Obviously, predictability is not something you can count on with variable annuities. Market fluctuations make that impossible.

 Consider This _____

> How comfortable are you with risk? If the thought of not knowing how much your variable annuity will pay bothers you, look for another way to fund your retirement.

Clearly, people who buy variable annuities are looking for something more than the fixed annuity or even the equity-indexed annuity has to offer.

That "something" is the opportunity to earn returns that far surpass any offered by traditional savings products. The price for this opportunity is the risk that you will lose money. This speaks to another reason people invest in annuities: supplements to their retirement plan or, in some cases, the entire retirement plan.

How They Work

Purchasing a variable annuity is more complicated than buying a regular fixed annuity—there are more forms to fill out and more decisions to make.

Variable annuities are registered securities, which means there is a prospectus involved, along with many rules and regulations the salesperson must follow. In addition, you will need to decide how much of your premium goes into the general account and how much goes into the separate accounts or subaccounts.

The Prospectus

A *prospectus* is a legal document required for the sale of any registered security. Before you can buy a variable annuity, the SEC requires the salesperson to give you a copy of the prospectus and go over the main points.

$ Financial Speak _____

A **prospectus** is a legal document that details the terms of the variable annuity. The SEC reviews and approves it for distribution and it must accompany any marketing material.

The prospectus outlines all the pertinent information about the contract, including all of the fees and charges. It details the risks associated with the annuity and discusses the issuer. If your salesperson doesn't want to discuss the prospectus, ask yourself why. If he doesn't want to give you one, you should find another salesperson.

Funding a Variable Annuity

Almost all variable annuities are deferred annuities with payout at some future date. Typically, an initial premium opens the account, and the owner makes subsequent deposits either as she can or on some systematic basis.

The owner must decide how to allocate funds flowing into the annuity. How much goes into the fixed account(s), and how much goes into the subaccounts? As market conditions change or your financial goals change, you can adjust these allocations.

However, be sure you understand the rules concerning transferring money between fixed accounts and subaccounts. There may be fees for moving money out of the fixed accounts if you want to do so before the guaranteed interest period is up.

Variable Annuities in Your Portfolio

Remember that fight we started at the beginning of this chapter? The role of a variable annuity, if any, in a person's financial plan goes to the heart of the argument.

Clearly, the life insurance industry sees variable annuities as retirement-funding vehicles and aggressively promotes them as such. With tax-deferred growth, no limits on investments, and no capital gains worries, investors can take advantage of the long-term growth potential available in the market.

The detractors say, why pay high fees and high taxes on distributions when there are better alternatives for funding your retirement?

Let's take a look at variable annuities in the qualified and nonqualified markets so you can be the judge.

Qualified

Variable annuities' most bitter foes sputter with disbelief upon finding one in a qualified retirement plan. Yet, many employer-sponsored plans, such as 401(k)s, offer variable annuities as one of the choices.

Critics point out that variable annuities carry tax deferral without being inside a qualified retirement plan. In fact, a variable annuity inside a qualified retirement plan must adhere to the plan's guidelines on contributions and distributions, which are always more restrictive. One of the main benefits of annuities is the lack of limits on contributions, something you lose when the annuity is within a qualified plan.

Many variable annuities carry high fees, which only dilute any benefit of tax deferral. These fees are in addition to the fees charged by the retirement plan itself, which means less money for your retirement.

From my perspective, I haven't heard a good argument for variable annuities inside qualified retirement plans, unless the employer has a very generous match. If your retirement plan has other alternatives, I suggest you explore those and, if you're interested in variable annuities, consider investing in one that is nonqualified.

> **It's Your Money** _____
>
> If your employer offers only a variable annuity as a qualified retirement plan, see if they are open to considering adding other options. If they match part or all of your contribution, it might offset the negatives of high fees.

Nonqualified

Critics use the same arguments for nonqualified variable annuities—high fees, high taxes on distributions, and questionable value of the death benefit.

Their argument is "Why not just invest directly in mutual funds?" If you consider only the hard evidence, they are probably right. Most people probably are better off investing directly—assuming that they have the time and expertise to pick a good set of mutual funds that will give them a balanced portfolio.

One of the services you get with a good variable annuity is a professionally structured selection of subaccounts (mutual funds) that cover a broad horizon of asset classes. This selection lets investors allocate their assets according to their financial goals and risk tolerance. Building a portfolio like this on your own is not easy. Your alternative is a managed account of some type, which will also carry a fee.

However, it seems to me that variable annuities have a broader emotional appeal than just a purely analytical decision. You can't ignore the sense of security associated with life insurance companies. For many people, they stand for stability and security—after all, we count on them being there to pay off when it's time to cash in a life insurance policy.

The comfort of knowing that, no matter how badly your investments do, you can pass on at least what you invested and perhaps a lot more is important to some people who otherwise would be reluctant about investing in the market.

Active Trader

Oddly enough, if you are a person who is an active mutual fund trader, you may find variable annuities attractive.

A variable annuity with a broad set of subaccounts gives you a sheltered environment to trade multiple times during the year without running up short-term capital gains tax bills, which can be as bad as ordinary income taxes.

Most variable annuities allow a certain number of switches each year without charge and then levy a fee for any over those. Make sure you understand the rules before buying into a contract and thoroughly research the subaccounts.

You can even jump to another company's annuity using a 1035 transfer, which I discussed earlier, as long as you watch out for surrender charges.

Careful

Although you might be able to avoid some taxes by actively trading inside a variable annuity, this is generally not a good idea. Active traders tend to chase the next hot trend and are usually wrong.

Variable Annuity Risks

The biggest risk, of course, is that you could lose money with a variable annuity. The argument that the death benefit can make your investment back does you precious little good when you are trying to make ends meet in retirement. The other big risk is that the fees, which may change with some annuities, could wipe out most of your gains.

Investment Risks

Any investment in the stock market carries risk—don't let salespeople tell you otherwise. They like to talk about historical returns and so on, but the truth is that averages are not reality. They are a mathematical function that smoothes out the highs and lows. What happens if you need your money when the market is at a low?

The chart that follows is the closing value of the S&P 500 Index on May 1 of each year listed. If you invested $1000 in a mutual fund that followed this index in 1998, you were doing pretty good by 2000—up 30 percent ($1090 up to $1420). However, what if you invested in 2000 and needed your money in 2003? Ouch, you were down 32 percent ($1420 down to $1107):

Year	1998	1999	2000	2001	2002	2003	2004
S&P 500	$1090	$1301	$1420	$1255	$1067	$963	$1107

This example illustrates two important points:

- Risks are associated with investing in variable annuities.
- An investment in a variable annuity is a long-term commitment. The longer you leave your money invested, the better chance you have to make it through the peaks and valleys that are a normal part of the stock market.

Potential for High Fees

The high fees of variable annuities can wipe out most of the gains in the subaccounts if you don't choose wisely. Variable annuities charge several different fees, which I discuss in depth in Chapter 10.

The important point here is that you shouldn't assume that all variable annuities charge about the same. This is not the case. It pays to shop around for an annuity that has the right combination of features and fees.

The Least You Should Know

- Variable annuities are controversial financial products that have strong supporters and opponents.
- Variable annuities have three components: the fixed account, the subaccounts, and the death benefit.
- Variable annuities are registered securities, and salespeople must give you a prospectus with marketing material.
- You can lose money investing in a variable annuity.

Variable Annuity Subaccounts

In This Chapter

- The "variable" part of variable annuities
- Subaccount basics
- Types of subaccounts
- Investment strategies

In this chapter, we look at the separate account portion of the variable annuity in depth. This is the "variable" part of variable annuities. Money flows through the separate account and into subaccounts.

If you know something about mutual funds, you are ahead of the game on subaccounts because that's all subaccounts are—mutual funds that insurance companies call by another name.

Investing is about risk and reward. Understanding this relationship and your level of risk tolerance will help you decide which, if any, variable annuity is right for you.

Where the Money Goes

When you make an initial variable annuity deposit, you decide how much of the premium goes to the general (fixed) account and how much goes to the separate account. Within the separate account are a number of subaccounts. Your next decision is to allocate your premium between one or more of those accounts.

If you've done your homework, you know that the variable annuity offers a range of subaccounts that meet your particular needs. I discuss the different types of subaccounts in the section "Types of Subaccounts."

The Conversion

Before we get any deeper, it might be helpful to discuss how the managers price subaccounts. With mutual funds, if you are familiar with calculating the net asset value (NAV), you probably already understand the pricing of subaccounts.

Subaccount pricing in the variable annuity industry uses a value called annuity accumulation unit value, or AUV. Managers calculate this value at the end of each day to give buyers and sellers a current price. Here's how the AUV is calculated:

Value of all securities	$10,000,000
Management fees	–$120,000
Expenses	–$80,000
Total	$9,800,000
Divide by the number of outstanding shares	500,000
Accumulated Unit Value (AUV)	$19.60

The movement of the AUV tells you how the sub-account is doing and whether you are making any money.

Unlike purchasing individual stocks, when you invest in mutual funds and subaccounts, you invest whole-dollar amounts rather than buying X number of shares. This means that you own fractional shares, something that is not likely with individual stocks.

Who Gets the Money

You might be surprised to know that the managers of the subaccounts don't actually get their hands on your money. The insurance company sends your premium to a transfer agent, who records your investment. The transfer agent then sends the money to a custodian bank, which notifies the subaccount manager that the money is available for investment.

These safeguards are in place to prevent any hanky panky with your funds. They also protect the life insurance company, because the money passes out of their responsibility.

Subaccount Basics

When a company decides to offer a variable annuity, it often contracts with a money-management firm to run the subaccounts. Almost all of the major mutual fund companies partner with life insurance companies in this way to offer their products through variable annuities. In many cases, they clone existing mutual funds into subaccounts for the variable annuity.

Subaccounts offer a variety of benefits for the investor, including professional management, diversification, and a range of investment opportunities.

Professional Management

One of the real benefits of investing in subaccounts is access to professional money managers. These are the people who run the subaccounts and are also known as "portfolio managers." They are highly trained and experienced market professionals who study the market on a daily basis.

They have access to volumes of information on individual companies and industry trends, and they have become experts in the market segment targeted by the subaccount.

Few of us have the time or expertise to match the attention they bring to the market. Investing in subaccounts allows you to tap into their expertise.

Diversification

Investing in subaccounts is a way to diversify your holdings. Diversification is another way of saying "Don't put all your eggs in one basket." Subaccounts invest in a large number of securities in their target asset class, while individual investors might be able to afford to own only a few stocks individually.

For example, a subaccount that focuses on large companies might own 100 or more individual stocks in its portfolio. If one or more of the stocks does poorly, it won't have a significant impact on the subaccount's total performance. It would take an individual of considerable means to match this type of portfolio, assuming that she had the expertise to pick the best 100 individual stocks out of the thousands available.

Range of Investment Options

Assuming that you have bought the right variable annuity, you have a range of investment opportunities in the subaccounts that match your level of risk tolerance. By adjusting the percentage of your investment between conservative and aggressive subaccounts, you can find that level of risk tolerance that is right for you.

Careful

If you put all of your money in one sub-account that invests in large companies, have you diversified your portfolio? The answer is no. You need to diversify over several different asset classes (such as cash, stocks, and bonds), as well as a large number of just one kind of investment.

This is another example of why it is important to do some homework and shopping before you purchase a variable annuity. If the subaccounts don't fit your risk profile, you aren't going to be comfortable with your investment.

At the risk of repeating and repeating myself, all variable annuities are not equal. There are significant differences in the quality and quantity of subaccounts offered by various variable annuities.

Subaccount Families

As with mutual fund families, subaccount families are groups of subaccounts offered together as a package to cover a wide range of investment goals and objectives. As with individual subaccounts, money managers thoughtfully construct these families with the investor in mind.

The idea is not entirely selfless. The subaccount managers want to make sure investors have a place to go within the family if their investment objectives change. This is why most subaccounts allow you a certain number of free switches each year within the family.

Subaccount families may look different from one variable annuity to another, but most will contain certain subaccounts as basics or foundations of the family.

Types of Subaccounts

Subaccounts attempt to address a wide variety of investment objectives. A well-constructed variable annuity will have a family of subaccounts that spans the investment spectrum in terms of size and asset classes.

As with mutual funds, you can classify subaccounts several ways, including by asset class and size of equities purchased. The sections that follow describe some sample subaccount classifications.

Growth Subaccount

The growth subaccount seeks capital appreciation (share growth). It invests in companies that have a better-than-average chance of growing in the current economic climate. Many of these companies don't pay dividends, electing instead to reinvest profits in the company to fuel further growth and increase share price.

This is typically an aggressive investment because some of the companies won't succeed and the subaccount will have to sell them off, perhaps at a loss.

How aggressive this subaccount is may depend on whether it further segments itself by company size. A subaccount that focuses on small-cap growth companies is a more aggressive and risky investment than a subaccount that invests in larger growth companies.

Value Subaccount

A value subaccount attempts to identify companies that the market is undervaluing for some reason. Perhaps the company is in an industry that is not in the spotlight currently, or the money manager sees something that she believes others have overlooked. In any case, value subaccounts don't invest in stocks because their price is low; they invest because they believe the company is worth more than the current share price reflects. When the market recognizes the true value of the company, it will reprice the stock, and the subaccount will make a profit.

Value subaccounts can also be categorized by size, which changes the relative level of risk. The risk with value subaccounts is that the market may never reprice the stock, or the money manager may discover that the real reason for the low price is something the company could not correct.

> **It's Your Money**
>
> Value investing lends itself to retirement accounts because it is typically a long-term hold, which suits the time frame of most folks building a retirement fund.

Income Subaccount

An investor looking for income from a variable annuity might find an income subaccount appealing. This particular account invests in a variety of income-producing equities and bonds, with the goal of high current income and capital appreciation.

These subaccounts might break down into bond subaccounts, along with others that invest in utility stocks and debt instruments. Purchases can range from U.S. Treasury instruments to lower-rated corporate bonds and dividend-paying stocks such as "blue chip" companies.

Index Subaccount

The index subaccount mimics the popular index mutual funds. Both follow one of the popular market indexes by buying the identical stocks that go into the index. The most popular index, as we have previously discussed, is the S&P 500 Index, which is a market-weighted index of 500 leading companies.

The index subaccount that follows the S&P 500 buys exactly the same stocks in the same percentage that makes up the index. The subaccount tracks the S&P 500 index almost perfectly. This allows an investor to "buy the market" for a very small price and is a good long-term investment.

Index subaccounts are relatively easy to manage. There are no investment decisions—they just do what the S&P 500 does, and they always announce when they make changes. This keeps management costs down. There are subaccounts based on other market indexes, and they all work the same way.

Global Subaccounts

Global subaccounts recognize the fact that our economy is part of and subject to global influences. These subaccounts invest in securities from around the world. Money managers look for investment opportunities in emerging economies that may be growing as fast as or faster than ours.

This type of investment is somewhat risky, but most professionals believe that a small portion of your money should be in this type of subaccount if you are building a retirement fund. If you are in capital-preservation mode, you might want to skip this sub-account.

Gold/Precious Metals Subaccount

For the sake of brevity, I have combined the gold and precious metals subaccounts into one category, but you will usually see them as separate entities. The idea is that gold and precious metals are historical inflation hedges. Gold, in particular, has long been the place money retreats to when inflation rears its ugly head.

Gold/precious metals subaccounts invest in stock and debt instruments of companies that mine and distribute these elements. They seldom hold the actual metals or gems. These subaccounts normally would only occupy a small percentage of your portfolio, but they can be the protection against inflation that many retirement plans lack.

Money Market Subaccount

The money market subaccount invests in short-term cash instruments, such as CDs, commercial paper (debt issued by corporations), and Treasury issues. The money market subaccount is the only one whose AUV does not change on a daily basis. The goal is to keep the AUV at $1 every day, which means the interest rate fluctuates on a daily basis. The money market subaccount will not pay as much as the fixed account in the general account, for example, and most people use it just to hold money for a short term before investing in another subaccount.

Others

I have not tried to do a comprehensive listing, but the subaccounts described represent the major groupings you will find in a well-constructed variable annuity. The literature probably will not give them the same names, but in the descriptive language, you will find that they likely fall into one of these broad categories.

For example, you may see a subaccount listed as "large-cap value" or "small-cap growth." This just tells you that the money manager has further segmented by company size.

How many subaccounts should a good variable annuity have? That depends on your investment objectives. That being said, an annuity with only two or three choices seems too constrained to me. On the other hand, 40 subaccounts is probably overkill. The best answer is enough to fit your financial needs.

 Consider This

> Financial professionals categorize companies by size using a capitalization ratio, which is the number of outstanding shares multiplied by the share price. A small-cap stock is $1 billion or less, a midcap stock is $1–$5 billion, and a large-cap stock is $5 billion plus.

Investing Strategies

One of the benefits of investing through a variable annuity is the investing strategies you can use to accomplish your goals. The strategies fall into two categories: external to the variable annuity and internal to the separate account.

These strategies range from the fairly simple to the more complex, and from the passive to the more involved. Not all annuities offer the strategies listed in the sections that follow. If you don't think you need or want them, don't bother looking for an annuity that offers them—they're not free.

Dollar Cost Averaging

Simply stated, with dollar cost averaging, you commit to investing a fixed amount (usually monthly) into a separate account, regardless of what the market is doing.

Here is how it works, assuming that you invested $300 per month into a variable annuity:

Month	Deposit	Unit Price	Units Purchased
1	$300	$14	21.42
2	$300	$12	25.00
3	$300	$16	18.75
4	$300	$19	15.79
5	$300	$21	14.28
6	$300	$20	15.00
	$1,800	$17	110.24
		Avg. Price	Total Units
Average cost per unit = $16.33			

When the market is up (Month 5), you buy fewer shares because the AUV is higher. When the market is down (Month 2), you buy more because the AUV is lower. In other words, you buy more when prices are low and less when prices are high. The result is a lower average price per unit over a period.

This may not seem like much of a savings; however, over 10 years, the difference is significant. Dollar cost averaging also works in a down market. The catch is, you must stick with it. Make a commitment to pay your retirement fund first, and don't waver. When you combine the savings of dollar cost averaging and the tax-deferred growth, you have a chance to build a substantial nest egg.

 Careful

> Dollar cost averaging will not guarantee you a profit. It is simply a way to buy shares at a lower average price. If the subaccount is going into the toilet, lower average prices won't help.

Another benefit of dollar cost averaging is that it takes the emotion out of investing. There are no decisions to make. You invest every month, regardless of what the market is doing. This helps you avoid chasing hot tips or panic selling when things look bad. I said earlier that averages were not reality, but if you stick with an investment program for the long term, you have a better chance that the historical returns of the stock market will work for you, not against you.

Switches

This is the ability to move money from one subaccount to another within the variable annuity. Most annuities allow you to make switches a certain number of times each year without charge. Once you pass that number, there may be a charge for additional switches.

Switching is not an investment strategy, but a way to accomplish a strategy. Moving money from one subaccount to another is fine if there is a well-thought-out reason for the move and it fits within an overall strategy. Don't do it just because you can.

Asset Allocation

This is the distribution of investment dollars according to your financial goals and risk tolerance. It involves figuring out a balance between stocks, bonds, and cash. If the idea of a professional money manager working with your investments sounds appealing, look for a variable annuity that offers this service. Some offer preset portfolios geared for a variety of circumstances, while others offer a more personalized service. In each case, expect to pay for the service, as you would in the investing world outside the variable annuity.

Portfolio Rebalancing

This service maintains a certain balance in your portfolio—say, between growth and income sub-accounts. If one of these subaccounts does very well, it will grow out of balance with the other. For example, your goal might be to have 60 percent of your money in growth and 40 percent in income, but the growth subaccount might have a good run and command 75 percent of the portfolio. Portfolio rebalancing would sell off enough of the growth subaccount and either buy more income or take that profit out of the annuity. Either way, it would bring the portfolio back into the 60/40 balance.

The Least You Should Know

- The annuity accumulation unit value (AUV) is how the industry prices variable annuity subaccounts.

- The benefits of investing in subaccounts include diversification, professional management, and a range of investment opportunities.

- Variable annuity subaccount categories include growth, income, value, global, gold, and money market.

- Investors in subaccounts have a number of investment strategies available to them, including dollar cost averaging, asset allocation, and portfolio rebalancing.

10

Variable Annuity Fees

In This Chapter

- What contract fees are
- Fees for separate accounts
- Subaccount fees and expenses
- Ways to battle high fees

The single biggest complaint about variable annuities is the high fees. Of course, *high* is always a relative term. High compared to what? Most of the time, the comparison is to mutual funds.

A fee is never high if you believe that it has purchased a reasonable value. However, you cannot make a decision about reasonable value if you don't understand what you are buying or how much it costs. This chapter takes a closer look at the fees associated with variable annuities so you can make an informed decision. Remember my ongoing caution: Variable annuities are not the same; it pays to shop for features and fees.

What You Pay

In almost any comparison between mutual funds and variable annuities on fees, the annuity will lose because of all the extra benefits and bells and whistles it offers. Whether you need or want those extras is your decision.

The industry is responding to the high-fee criticism with some low-cost products, but the bulk of the market remains priced higher than straight mutual funds. As long as the commissions remain high on the sale of variable annuities, we'll continue to see relatively high fees.

The fees you pay break down into three main areas: general contract fees (the bulk of your fees), separate account fees, and subaccount fees. Each is described in this chapter.

General Contract Fees

Variable annuities carry higher administrative and maintenance costs than mutual fund accounts because of the dual nature of the product. The general account stays with the life insurance company, and the separate account funds the subaccounts by routing money through a *transfer agent*.

However, the biggest ongoing single fee is the mortality and expense risk charge. This expense, which includes the death benefit, takes a serious nip out of your account on an annual basis—be sure the death benefit has some value to you.

> **$ Financial Speak** _____
>
> A **transfer agent** handles the recording of new investors and maintains records for the company of investors in the subaccounts.

Surrender charges are the other big expense and happen only if you surrender your contract early. Depending on how the contract structures the charges and when you surrender the contract, you could pay a hefty charge.

Account Maintenance Fees

As you might imagine if you have ever dealt with an insurance company, paperwork is always involved with variable annuities. The company has to keep up-to-date vital information about the contract holder, beneficiaries, and so on. The company must process statements, and the general busy work of administering a complicated financial product costs money.

Most variable annuities charge a flat fee, usually on the anniversary date and when you surrender the annuity. The fees run around $25 to $35 per year, but always check; you can find them higher and lower.

M&E Expense Risk Fee

The mortality and expense risk (M&E) charges pay the insurance premium to cover the death benefit and then some. Part of this fee goes to pay for the insurance necessary to guarantee the death benefit, and part goes to cover expenses that might exceed the administrative service charges (more about them in a minute).

This expense splits into two components: the insurance portion and the company's slush fund to make sure it covers all its costs. Some companies split these two when detailing fees; others report them as a single figure.

> ### It's Your Money
>
> Just as with adding extras on to a new car, those optional benefits can drive up fees in a hurry. Make sure you really need the extra features before you add them to the contract.

The mortality or death benefit charge is all over the board, but it averages something over 1.1 percent of the account value. If you add some of the extra death benefit options, this number could climb dramatically. Even at 1.1 percent, it takes $1,100 a year out of a $100,000 account—pricey for an insurance policy. Actually, it's probably more than $1,100. Many companies deduct this from your account on a daily basis by annualizing the interest rate.

In addition to covering expenses not paid by the administration fee, the company may use the administrative expense portion to pay sales commissions on the product. Anything left over goes into the company's pocket.

Surrender Charges

Although this is not technically a fee, it is very important for you to understand a contract's surrender charges. Sometimes called "deferred sales charges" or "contingent sales charges," these fees hit you if you surrender the contract early.

You may find some contracts with no surrender charges, but most variable annuities have them ranging from 5 to 15 years. Typically, the charges start high and decrease annually down to zero. If you surrender the contract before the charges expire, you'll pay the prevailing surrender charge on your account balance.

This is especially true on 1035 transfers, which we talked about in Chapter 5. You may be tempted to move out of one variable annuity and into another, but you had best check the status of surrender charges first. If it costs you 5 percent of your account value to move, you had better be moving out of a really bad situation because it will take a long time to recover that much money. Almost certainly, you will start a new surrender period with any new annuity.

Separate Account Fees

One of the fees that most contracts list is the administrative fee, which covers the cost of handling the business of the separate account. It is a percentage of the value of the separate account.

Among the items it covers is transferring funds from one subaccount to another or out of the general account. Reports—quarterly, semiannually, or yearly—also must be processed and distributed.

 Careful

> Watch out for salespeople who make a big deal about the guarantee on a little fee, but gloss over the fact that the larger fees are way out of line. It is easy to guarantee a small fee when you are over-charged somewhere else.

Many companies guarantee that this fee will not exceed a certain amount. They can do this because of the M&E risk charge, which provides extra money if expenses exceed this fee. This fee is all over the board, and you should look at it in relation to the M&E risk charge. I don't have a good sense of the average, but don't be surprised by 0.20 percent or higher.

Subaccount Fees

We're not finished with fees yet. This set of fees deals with the management of the subaccounts. Incidentally, these fees are similar to those you would pay a mutual fund company to manage your money.

The company that manages the subaccounts doesn't work free, and expenses are associated with buying and selling stocks and bonds. These expenses come out of the investor's funds. However, investors never see a bill for management fees and subaccount fees—they come out of the total invested funds in the subaccounts before the AUV is calculated.

Management Fees

Management fees cover the cost of the portfolio of money managers who manage the various subaccounts. Frequently, a life insurance company contracts with a mutual fund company to manage the subaccount for its variable annuity product. The fees can run all over the place, depending on the type of subaccounts in the separate account. For example, money market subaccounts and index subaccounts are less expensive for mutual fund companies to manage than global subaccounts.

The mutual fund company charges a fee that applies to how much money is in the subaccount. Overall, management fees average around 0.85 percent of assets under management. A company that manages several subaccounts would charge different fees for each subaccount, depending on the expertise required to run the subaccount.

Although you don't see these costs on a bill anywhere, they have a direct impact on your return. The lower your costs are, the better chance you have of earning a decent return on your investment. You don't have to be a math whiz to see the wisdom of keeping all of your expenses as low as possible without giving up those benefits and features that are important to you.

Subaccount Expenses

It costs the management company money to buy and sell stocks and bonds, and the companies pass on those expenses to the investors in the subaccount. They must pay transaction costs, brokerage fees, and other expenses in the course of managing the subaccount.

As with management fees, these expenses vary, depending on the type of subaccount. The expenses for a money market subaccount may not run any higher than 0.05 to 0.10 percent. On the other hand, a subaccount that invests in foreign securities may face expenses of 0.75 to 1.00 percent of funds under management.

It's Your Money _____

When you choose the subaccounts to invest in, you should get details of each one's management fees. Expect to see some differences.

How It Adds Up

It is hard to say what a typical variable annuity costs in terms of fees because there isn't a "standard" product across providers. However, we can look at some averages and benchmarks for your reference, with the understanding that the variable annuity market is quite dynamic and competitive, which can drive fees up or down.

Morningstar.com is a great source for information on all types of investments. Check its site for the latest news on variable annuities, but be warned: They are not big fans of the product, because of fees.

If there is an average variable annuity out there, expect to pay about 2.25 to 2.35 percent in total expenses. If you add on some of the more sophisticated death benefits and other riders, expect that number to go up.

Remember, you may not see all those expenses on a statement anywhere. The subaccount fees come out of the invested funds, so you never see that money. However, it is a definite drag on the subaccount's performance. On a $100,000 account, these fees could suck out more than $2,000 a year. Of course, this doesn't include any surrender charges if you pull out too soon, which could wipe out a big chunk of any gain or make a loss even worse.

Let's look at an example of how fees affect your return:

Account value	$100,000
Plus return (8%)	+$8,000
Total	$108,000
Minus fees (2.3%)	–$2,484
Net	$105,518 (+5.5%)

Not a pretty picture. You can see from this simple illustration that fees can have a devastating effect on the return. In addition, they can become extremely painful when your subaccounts are also losing money. It takes a strong will to ride out market fluctuations.

Overcoming the Fee Deficit

Proponents of variable annuities argue that the tax-deferred growth of the subaccounts offsets the high fees when compared with mutual funds, which must pay taxes each year on short-term gains and distributions. Not surprisingly, they can construct scenarios in which variable annuities are a better deal than regular mutual funds. Their charts and graphs show how the variable annuity wins thanks to its tax-deferred growth, even with the weight of its high fees.

On the other side, opponents roll out their charts and graphs that show the exact opposite—that there is no way variable annuities win against mutual funds with lower fees and no ordinary income tax on distributions.

My grandfather used to say, "Figures lie and liars figure." I'm not accusing anyone of lying, but by constructing the scenario properly, you can influence the results.

You can overcome—or at least mitigate—the high fees of variable annuities in three ways:

- Shop around for the annuity that combines the features you want with reasonable fees.

- Consider one of the low-cost variable annuity providers.

- Plan to hold your variable annuity for 10 to 15 years or more.

Do Some Shopping

If you believe a variable annuity is for you, do some shopping before you get out your checkbook. This is a big commitment, and you owe it to yourself to get the annuity that works best for you.

The Internet has a number of resources to get you started (refer to Appendix B for a list of websites with helpful information). You can get information on variable annuities sent to you, but because they are registered securities, you can't get the information anonymously.

Low-Cost Alternatives

Some of the leaders in the low-cost mutual fund world have introduced their answer to the high fees of traditional variable annuities. These fund companies, which carved out a major niche in the mutual fund industry, applied their cost-cutting mentality to variable annuities. They have come up with some interesting alternatives.

These variable annuities are worth a close look if you're not interested in all the bells and whistles.

They are more "stripped-down" versions of the product than regular offerings, but that may suit your needs just fine, and the price is certainly better.

 Consider This

> Your financial adviser may not be too keen on discussing these low-cost alternatives. Many of the companies offer them directly to the consumer. However, they are certainly worth a look.

One of the features that is missing from some (but not all) of the low-cost options is the guaranteed interest that traditional variable annuities offer in the general account. If you invest in one of these variable annuities, you are giving up any guaranteed income from the contract. What you are getting is an investment in the stock market that grows in a tax-deferred environment with a life insurance policy that provides some protection of principal.

Vanguard and T. Rowe Price, two mutual fund leaders known for their low-cost products, are worth looking at for their variable annuity products. With expenses less than 1 percent (compared to more than 2 percent for regular variable annuities), these two and other low-cost providers offer worthy alternatives for people who can live without the full complement of features.

You might be wondering how a mutual fund company like Vanguard can offer a variable annuity that is supposed to be a life insurance product. Simple: It pairs up with an existing life insurance company that provides the death benefit portion of the contract—the reverse of a life insurance company contracting with a money manager to provide funds management.

Hold on Tight

Variable annuities are definitely a long-term investment. The longer you hold the annuity, the harder the tax-deferred growth works for you, and this is what helps offset the high fees.

In the ideal world, you would open the account in your early 50s and hold it for 15 or 20 years before touching it. This would give it a long time to grow while you were making regular contributions (monthly). Even the financial professionals who don't like variable annuities agree that the longer you hold them, the better they look in comparison to mutual funds.

If you expect to begin withdrawals in a few years, variable annuities are probably not for you—consider a fixed annuity or some other financial instrument.

The Bottom Line

You will probably pay more for a variable annuity than for a comparable set of mutual funds, but certain features in the annuity could make that extra cost worthwhile to you.

There is nothing wrong with paying for the security you may feel with a variable annuity or the benefit of tax-deferred growth.

Controlling expenses is important, but it is not the only consideration. You should look at the whole picture and make your decision based on all of the factors, not just fees alone.

The Least You Should Know

- Mortality and expense risk charge is one of the biggest fees associated with variable annuities.

- Subaccount fees cover the expenses of the money-management company.

- Fees have a devastating impact on account value.

- Consider a low-cost variable annuity.

Picking Variable Annuities

In This Chapter

- Maybe you shouldn't own a variable annuity
- Deciding what's important
- Rating providers
- Understanding returns and payouts

Were you surprised at the first bullet point above? If you remember the introduction, the purpose of this book is to give you the information you need to make an informed decision about variable annuities. I never said they were right for everyone.

If you believe that a variable annuity might fit your personal financial needs, how do you go about finding one? More than likely, they will come looking for you—at least, people selling them will find you.

How do you rate a provider? This is a long-term commitment, and you are counting on the provider to be there when you need to start reaping some of your hard-earned rewards.

Speaking of rewards, how do you monitor your progress? What do you need to know about variable annuity returns and payout options to plan for that time when it comes? Read on.

Are You a Good Candidate?

Despite what you may hear from salespeople, not everyone is a good candidate for a variable annuity. In fact, if you listen to some financial professionals, they believe only a tiny fraction of the population is a good candidate.

The truth is probably somewhere in between those two extreme points of view. The only real issue that concerns you is whether you believe a variable annuity fits your financial needs. If you get to this point in the book and conclude that they are just not you, then you have saved yourself from a very expensive mistake—good for you for not following the crowd and for making up your own mind.

Here are some points to help you decide whether you are a good candidate for a variable annuity:

- Time frame
- Risk tolerance
- Importance of passing something on

I am assuming you want to build on a retirement nest egg, but any number of products can help you accomplish that goal. The question before you is whether a variable annuity is one of those products.

Time Frame

All investing should be a long-term affair, but this is particularly true of variable annuities. It is important to make a long-term commitment to a variable annuity for two reasons:

- The longer the holding period is, the more the tax-deferred growth offsets the high fees.
- The risk factor of any investment in the stock market goes down the longer you stay in the market.

Depending on how high the fee is for a variable annuity, the holding period to offset it may extend 10–15 or more years. By offsetting the fee, I mean relative to a comparable investment in mutual funds without tax-deferred growth. All things being equal, the tax-deferred growth will eventually overcome the drag of the fees associated with the variable annuity. (Remember, even so-called "no-load" mutual funds also have fees that drag on their performance.)

I have already noted that there are many legitimate reasons to pay the high fees, so entirely offsetting them may not be a driving reason for holding an investment. However, it can't hurt.

A bigger concern is the notorious fluctuations of the stock market and the havoc they can wreak over a short period. However, you take a great deal of risk out of investing by staying in the market with a properly balanced portfolio for a long period—ideally, 15 years or more.

 **Careful** _____

> Make sure you have sufficient cash flow for your everyday expenses, plus a reserve to cover emergencies, before undertaking a long-term investment program.

If you don't feel that you can commit to a program of systematic investment for a period of no less than five years and hopefully 15 years or more, look for something else to help fund your retirement. That "something else" shouldn't be anything based on the stock market—look to a fixed annuity, a bank CD, and so forth.

Risk Tolerance

I call this "the good night's sleep" test. If you are going to worry so much about your investment in a variable annuity (that is, the stock market) that it will keep you awake at night, it's the wrong investment for you.

There is no shame in acknowledging that with your level of risk tolerance you are not comfortable with a stock market investment. The media wants to make heroes out of risk takers, but most of us don't fit comfortably in that category. Your discomfort with investing may come from a lack of understanding, in which case, you may want to do some more research to see if that brings up your level of risk tolerance. If not, you can save for your retirement in many ways without buying a variable annuity or investing money in a financial product that you don't understand or trust.

On the plus side, variable annuities provide a floor for you if it is important to preserve something for the next generation. No matter how badly your investments do, the death benefit can recover your investment for your heirs under the worst of circumstances (see the next section). In this sense, variable annuities take the risk out of investing.

Importance of Passing Something On

I talked about this in Chapter 4 and in several other places in the book, but it can be a critical factor in determining whether you are a candidate for a variable annuity.

If your goal in life is to run out of heartbeats about the same time you run out of money, you are probably not a candidate for a variable annuity. If you don't have any interest in passing on anything to heirs, why pay for an expensive death benefit? As noted in the previous chapter, the fee for this benefit (that you don't need) takes a big bite out of your return.

On the other hand, if you want to leave your beneficiary something when you're gone, there are other ways besides a variable annuity to accomplish the goal. Estate planning is beyond the scope of this book, but if you anticipate a sizable estate, variable annuities are probably not the best vehicle for passing on assets. You need the services of a qualified estate planner (CPA, attorney, or Certified Financial Planner).

The middle position where most of us reside wants the benefits of potentially high returns with the knowledge that if we run out of heartbeats earlier than anticipated, our beneficiary will have something left.

The reality of retirement planning involves couples, and with variable annuities, when one dies, the survivor can continue the contract, if it is set up correctly. This keeps your money in the market working for the survivor, who can make the appropriate decision regarding its disposition without the hassle of probate.

> **It's Your Money** _____
>
> Be sure you and your spouse are on the same page when it comes to your retirement plan and what you want or don't want to leave to the kids.

What's Important to You

Variable annuities can address several problems for people preparing for retirement, with good results. Other products can also address these problems, but let's look at how variable annuities can help with three of the big ones.

First and foremost is the problem of taxes. If you are trying to build a retirement fund, taxes will just keep pulling you back down the hill.

Another problem for many people is that they want market returns on part of their retirement funds, but they lack the risk tolerance to go naked into the market.

The final problem is for the individual who is way behind on funding retirement and needs to play serious catch-up.

Taxes

This is an easy problem to spot. If you have maxed out all your potential qualified retirement plans and find yourself with a tax bill at the end of the year on additional retirement savings, you should consider an annuity. If your risk tolerance is so inclined, a variable annuity may be the answer. If not, a fixed annuity solves the tax problem just as well and performs better, in most cases, than traditional savings instruments (bank CDs, for example).

Market Returns

Most financial experts agree that it is hard to build a retirement fund and stay ahead of inflation without some of your assets in the stock market. Yet, some people find the thought of investing in the market nerve-wracking. As such, the provider of variable annuities has already done the homework for you and selected the money manager for the subaccounts, so you don't have to choose from 10,000 mutual funds (literally)—you can select only from the subaccounts offered.

In addition, variable annuities can put a floor of confidence under such investors with a death benefit that says if something happens, the beneficiary will, at least, get the premium back under the right circumstances.

Catch-up

As discussed earlier in the book, some baby boomers were more interested in immediate gratification than planning for retirement. As a result, they are seriously behind in building their retirement nest egg.

If you have maxed out your retirement accounts or, in some cases, had limited access to retirement accounts, annuities are the only way to sock away large sums of money in a tax-deferred account. Because there is no limit on contributions unless the life insurance company imposes one, you can shovel in as much money as you can afford. You could do the same thing with a mutual fund, but you would also face a yearly tax bill.

Choosing a Provider

How do you go about choosing a provider for a variable annuity? Throughout this book, I have

talked about the life insurance company as the
provider, and that is technically correct. Life insurance companies offer annuities, but you will see
numerous other financial service companies hawking
their own variable annuities. How can this be?

It can't, technically. If you look carefully, all of these
providers work with a life insurance company, one
either under their corporate umbrella or through
a marketing agreement with an outside company.
Vanguard, the mutual fund giant, offers a variable
annuity through Peoples Benefit Life Insurance
Company of Cedar Rapids, Iowa.

Regardless of whose name is on the front, the life
insurance company writes the contract. It guarantees
the fixed interest rate in the general account and the
death benefit. However, the life insurance company
has no responsibility for the separate account (that's
why it's called "separate"). You need to look to the
mutual fund company or money manager that handles the subaccounts for that accountability. As such,
this involves checking on both the life insurance
company and the money manager. This complicates
matters somewhat, because you need to do two
checks rather than one: Both providers must pass.

Rating the Life Insurance Company

As we discussed in the section "Value of
'Guarantee'" in Chapter 1, several independent
services keep tabs on the financial strength of insurance companies. Just because you haven't heard of a
company doesn't mean it is not rock solid—it may

just mean that it doesn't spend millions on advertising. However, a sound rating is not the whole story. That just tells you that the company is not likely to fold any time soon. You should also be interested in what the company's customer service is like.

Almost certainly, a salesperson will sell you a variable annuity; however, as the years go by, you will deal with additional insurance company personnel in matters of customer service. This will involve the telephone, mail, and perhaps online activity.

If you follow my advice about long-term investing, you are entering a lengthy relationship with this company. You don't want to do business with an organization that screws up your statement every quarter or can't get a change of address right—what's going to happen when you need a really important transaction?

Here are a couple of other things to consider: How long does it take to talk to a real person on the phone? Do they have a website? Is it helpful? Can you view your account balances and conduct business?

Rating the Money Manager

Unfortunately, there are no rating companies for money managers and mutual fund companies as there are for life insurance companies. You are on your own. The typical rating is based on past performance—how much money they make for their investors. Before you get to the point of looking at performance, check out the quantity and quality of the company's subaccounts.

Quantity of Subaccounts

If the money manager doesn't offer the quantity of subaccounts you want, move on to another company. But how many subaccounts is right? There is no absolute right answer: However, 2 or 3 is not nearly enough, and 40 may be too many. Look for enough to cover the categories of investments discussed in Chapter 9. Keep in mind that the number of subaccounts by itself doesn't tell the whole story.

Quality of Subaccounts

The quality of subaccounts may sound a little fuzzy, but what I mean by this is that you need to determine the depth of investments offered. Do the subaccounts cover the three major asset classes of cash, stocks, and bonds? Do you have the choice of investment styles: value, income, and blended subaccounts? What about company size—are there subaccounts segmented by cap size? Are global and gold/precious metals subaccounts available? All of these categories give you options to build a portfolio that meets your particular needs.

Performance History

Performance history for subaccounts should go back at least five years. This is so you can see how the subaccount reacted through various market conditions. By the way they are designed, some subaccounts suffer in one market and thrive in another, while another subaccount may shoot for a more even performance across different markets.

All subaccounts should have a market index as a target. Many equity subaccounts use the S&P 500 Index as a measuring stick and report each year whether they "beat the market." Make sure the index chosen is appropriate for the subaccount so the measurement means something. For example, a small-cap value subaccount would need another index besides the S&P 500 Index to see whether it was beating its market.

> ### It's Your Money
>
> Here are some more questions to consider: Does the money manager offer asset-allocation portfolio services? What about portfolio rebalancing either within an asset-allocation model or as a stand-alone service? What other services does the money manager offer that will help you accomplish your goals?

Individual Money Managers

In the rarified atmosphere of financial services professionals, money managers who consistently make money are treated like rock stars (and are paid about the same). Though you may never have heard their names, "winners" are well known and highly compensated for their expertise. However, even the best don't have a winning year every year. The market has a humbling way of reminding the experts that it has a mind of its own.

Not only is it important to tie performance to a manager over a period of time, but this can also tell you whether the manager has weathered several different markets. You should look for managers who have been with a subaccount for several years at least, so you can tie historical performance to that individual. If the manager is new, historical performance of the fund may not mean much.

Subaccount Performance

A subaccount's performance depends on many factors, which makes predicting the future problematic, at best. It is possible for a subaccount to gain 15–20 percent a year or more, and it is equally possible to lose that much. The possibility of that gain attracts people to the market. You can't—and shouldn't—expect those types of returns every year, any more than you should expect those types of losses.

Taken as a whole, the stock market has returned an average of 10 to 12 percent a year over its history. That includes the Depression years of the 1920s, as well as the boom years of the late 1990s. This is the reason I cautioned earlier that you take much of the risk out of the market by staying invested over a long period. History supports this statement.

> **Careful**
>
> Avoid the "talking heads" of cable financial news, if possible, because they make every trading day on the market sound like it is the most important day in the history of stock trading. It isn't.

The biggest danger when gauging subaccount performance is to look at a very short-term view and make changes based on blips in performance. If you have done your homework, you shouldn't have to look at subaccount performance more than quarterly and make a thorough assessment annually. Clearly, if a subaccount has fallen behind and is not showing any signs of catching up, it might be time for a change, but not because it dipped last Thursday.

Variable Annuity Payouts

Variable annuity owners have all the same payout options available to them that we discussed in previous chapters, plus some that are unique. Obviously, you can convert your whole account through annuitization and take advantage of the traditional payouts. However, variable annuities have two annuitization components—fixed and variable—that make for some different payout configurations.

Most variable annuities have a general account with one or more fixed annuities. A common payout strategy is to link a regular fixed annuitization plan with the variable payout, to provide a predictable income stream to complement the variable income stream. For all the payout options with fixed annuities, refer back to Chapter 6.

With a variable annuitization payout option, you make an assumption about the rate of growth (for example, 5 percent) of the subaccounts, based on current market conditions. The company converts the AUVs into a monthly payment. Every month, the company bases your payment on the same number of AUVs, but their value will have changed either up or down, so your payment will rise or fall accordingly.

This means that the performances of the underlying subaccounts determine your monthly payment. If you find yourself falling behind, you can make adjustments. However, the idea is that this payout should help your income keep pace with inflation over the long term.

The Least You Should Know

- Not everyone is a good candidate for a variable annuity.
- Variable annuities can help you with problems related to taxes, catching up on your retirement fund, and potentially earning market returns with some security.
- In picking a variable annuity provider, you must be comfortable with not only the insurance company, but also the money manager.
- You should gauge subaccount performance on a long-term basis.

12

Risks of Variable Annuities

In This Chapter

- What is investment risk?
- What if tax laws change?
- Can you handle high-pressure sales?
- Are there early-distribution risks?

This is not a chapter about why you shouldn't buy a variable annuity. The fact that consumers bought more than $985 billion worth in variable annuities in 2003 is quite an endorsement for a product that some financial professionals believe to be a rip-off.

Even though I touched on risks in earlier chapters, I believe it is in your best interest to understand the more extreme risks associated with variable annuities so you can make up your own mind.

Investment Risk

You can lose money in the stock market. It happens every day, and it could happen to you. The market goes up, and the market goes down. It's that simple. The problem is, no one knows exactly when it will be up and when it will be down.

Even financial professionals don't know exactly what the market is going to do over any extended period.

History and Averages

Numerous times in this book, I have noted that you take much of the risk out of the market by staying invested over a long period. Based on market history, that is a correct statement. However, there is no way to say for sure that the market will act the same way in the future that it has acted in the past.

Averages aren't reality, and while you can take some comfort in working *with* the averages rather than *against* them, they offer no guarantee of investing success. Your safest course is always with the flow of how the market should act based on its history, but there are no guarantees.

 **Consider This**

> No one anticipated an event like the terrorists' attacks of September 11, 2001 and the effect they would have on the stock market.

Poor Choices

Even if the market continues to act in basically the same way as the past, what happens if you need to start pulling money out when the market is in a slump? Will you be able to wait until it rebounds?

You can make exactly the wrong choices in subaccounts for prevailing market conditions, or the money manager may do a terrible job. In either case, you can lose money that may be hard to recover.

Tax Law Risk

The variable annuity remains a viable product for one reason only: the tax-deferred growth it offers. Without the tax-deferred status, the product has no advantage in the market. On more than one occasion, politicians have discussed eliminating the tax-deferred status of annuities as a way to raise revenue.

Obviously, this would destroy the market. I doubt this will happen, given the trillions of dollars invested in all types of annuities. If it did happen, any existing annuities would more than likely retain their tax-deferred status.

The other tax issues include a further lowering of the capital gains tax, which makes straight mutual funds investing more attractive. In the late 1990s, Congress lowered the capital gains tax to the current 20 percent, and many people thought it would kill variable annuities. Clearly, it didn't, but it did make them less competitive with mutual funds.

The result is that you must now hold a variable annuity up to 15 years or longer, depending on its fee in a comparison with a mutual fund, to break even. If the capital gains rate drops further, it will just make it harder to justify a variable annuity over a mutual fund in a straight return comparison.

> **It's Your Money** _____
>
> Most people assume their income will be lower in retirement and that their income taxes will be also. This means you may pay a low tax rate on income from variable annuities.

An increase in income taxes could also put annuities at a further disadvantage because distributions get taxed under these rates. A lower capital gains tax rate and higher personal income tax rate—not an impossible scenario—would spell double trouble for variable annuities.

High-Pressure Sales Risk

One of the biggest risks in the variable annuity market is the danger of salespeople pressuring consumers into inappropriate decisions.

Earlier, I said consumers bought $985 billion in variable annuities. What I should have said is that salespeople sold consumers $985 billion in variable annuities in 2003. The industry pays very high commissions—5 percent and more—so it is not surprising that sales are brisk.

As noted earlier, variable annuities are registered securities, and only properly licensed professionals can sell them. Part of the salesperson's responsibility is to determine whether the product is suitable for the individual. If it is not, the salesperson should not sell that person the product.

There have been many complaints about variable annuity salespeople using high-pressure tactics to get people to buy, even if the product was not appropriate. Regulators from the SEC and NASD conducted inspections of more than 100 investment firms over a two-year period and found numerous abuses.

Among the problems they found were brokers making unsuitable recommendations and failure to disclose fees, risks, and potential tax liabilities. Some of the tactics included encouraging people to mortgage their homes to buy variable annuities (never do this), flipping annuities, and performing other tactics without warning the consumer of potential surrender fees or other problems.

Early Distribution Risk

Variable annuities are long-term investments. To make sure you understand that point, the government and life insurance companies load the product with huge penalties if you have to pull out your money prematurely.

Despite our best intentions, life happens. Without warning, you might need that $100,000 sitting in the variable annuity—and you might need it now. When cousin Fred talked you into dumping the profits from the sale of your late mother's house into the variable annuity, it sounded like a great idea. Now you wish you had thought about it some more.

When you pull out the money, Uncle Sam will take $10,000 off the top because you are not over 59½. The life insurance company is going to take $7,000 in surrender charges, leaving you with $83,000.

What's the lesson here? Variable annuities should never be more than 20 percent of your retirement plan, because they are not liquid until you are ready to annuitize them. Until then, you need a source of liquid capital to handle everyday expenses and an emergency cash reserve for the unexpected.

You fell victim to your own greed and an unscrupulous salesperson when you tied up all of the cash in a variable annuity. Any registered representative who encourages you to dump all of your retirement savings into a variable annuity is committing an unethical act, at best, and may be subject to disciplinary action.

Passing on Taxes

Variable annuities involve other problems, including passing on all those taxes you deferred to your heirs when you die. Of course, in some cases, that might bring a certain amount of perverse pleasure, but most of us don't want our heirs to remember us for the tax bills we left them.

If you plan to pass on a sizable estate to your heirs, sit down with a financial or estate planner before you buy a variable annuity, and discuss how it may or may not work in an overall plan.

> ### It's Your Money
>
> If your spouse is still alive, he or she can take over ownership of the variable annuity and keep going as if nothing happened. Problems arise when it passes to the next generation. Because annuities are outside the estate and probate, they go directly to the beneficiary along with a tax bill regardless of estate size.

Time Commitment

Although I don't want you to watch the value of your account go up or down on a daily basis, you do need to spend more time and pay more attention to a variable annuity than other types of annuities or savings investments.

Not only do you need to monitor your progress on a regular basis (quarterly is fine), but you should also keep an eye on your account statements and mail from the money manager and insurance company to make sure everything is in order. You also need to watch for fee increase notices and other account changes that might impact your subaccount's performance.

Expensive Riders

As with other annuities, variable annuities often offer riders on the contract for additional benefits. One of the most popular is the long-term care or nursing home benefit. This rider pays a certain amount for nursing home care. This is a scare sale because everyone over the age of 65 has heard horror stories about the cost of nursing home care.

However, does the rider provide adequate coverage for the price, or could you obtain coverage at a better price elsewhere? Don't assume that the rider offers any bargain—when is the last time an insurance company gave anything away?

Separate riders often pay extra-high commissions, so salespeople have a real incentive to push them, whether there is any benefit for you or not.

The Least You Should Know

- You can lose money in the stock market.
- Changes in the tax law could adversely affect your variable annuity.
- High-pressure salespeople may say anything to get you to buy.
- You may need to take an early distribution if you haven't planned carefully.

Glossary

12b-1 distribution fees   Charged to shareholders by the mutual fund company to provide for advertising and marketing, as well as "distribution" costs.

401(k) plan   A qualified defined contribution plan offered by employers. It allows employees to have a certain percentage of their salary deducted and invested in the plan. The deduction is pretax, so employees experience a reduction in current income tax. The plan usually has a number of mutual funds in which the employee can designate his deduction to be applied. In some cases, the employer may match a portion of the employee's contribution. The deposits and earnings are tax deferred until they are withdrawn in retirement.

403(b) plan   Similar to the 401(k) plan, the 403(b) is the retirement plan for religious, educational, and other nonprofit groups. This plan is a tax-deferred annuity plan because the investments must be annuities.

accumulation phase   Describes the period in which the owner is putting money into the contract, before annuitization.

administrative fees   Fees charged to maintain and administer a fund.

annuitant   The person the life insurance company uses as the base for the annuity payments. In most cases, the owner and the annuitant are the same person, but this doesn't have to be the case.

annuity   A periodic payment of equal amounts over a period of time. *Annuity* also refers to a contract with a life insurance company guaranteeing a certain payout over a period. It may contain a death benefit that would pay a survivor in the case of death.

asset allocation   The process of distributing your investment assets among different classes of investments in a manner that is consistent with your investment goals.

back-end load fund   A fund that charges a sales fee when you sell your shares.

beneficiary   The contract owner names a beneficiary or beneficiaries to receive the death benefit.

bonds   Debt instruments that represent an obligation on the part of the issuer to repay the debt. Governments and private corporations may issue bonds.

capital gain   The profit from the sale of an asset. Capital gain is realized when you sell a stock or

bond for a profit and when a mutual fund/
subaccount does the same. Capital gain passes on
to mutual fund shareholders, but not to subaccount
owners. Any asset sold for a profit and held less
than one year is subject to ordinary income tax by
the owner. This is a short-term capital gain. An
asset held for more than one year and sold for a
profit is a long-term capital gain, and the tax is 20
percent.

capital preservation strategy   Value preservation
of capital above return. An ultra-conservative strategy often used to pass a large "corpus" or body of a
trust to the next generation.

cash equivalents   Financial instruments that represent a deposit of cash. They include certificates
of deposit, money market accounts, and savings
accounts. These are highly liquid.

certificates of deposit   Banks issue certificates
of deposit. They have a maturity ranging, for the
most part, from six months to five years, and they
pay a fixed interest rate. There can be penalties for
withdrawing the money early.

Certified Financial Planner   A professional des-
ignation of someone who has extensive training in
financial planning. Many Certified Financial
Planners charge a fee only for their services, while
others may take a commission from products they
recommend you buy.

commissions   Fees brokers charge to buy or sell
securities for you.

common stock   The primary unit of ownership in a corporation. Holders of common stock are owners of the corporation, with certain rights, including voting on major issues concerning the corporation. Shareholders, as they are known, have liability limited to the value of the stock they own.

compounding   The mathematical means by which interest earned during one period adds to the principal. The next period, interest is earned on the resulting principal plus interest in the first period. Another way to say this is interest earning interest.

convertible bonds   Convertible bonds carry a feature that allows the owner to convert the bond to common stock instead of paying it off with cash.

death benefit   The contract pays the death benefit to the beneficiary upon the death of the annuity contract owner. Several optional death benefits may increase the payout.

defined benefit plan   The defined benefit plan states what the ultimate benefit will be in advance. This is typically a company pension plan. The years of service determine the benefit and some average the last three years' salary.

defined contribution plan   Plans that specify the contribution, but not the benefit. These plans focus on what goes into the plan and who contributes what. How much the plans will pay on retirement is dependent on the return earned by the plan.

diversification   The calculated spreading of your investments over a number of different asset classes. This cushions your portfolio if one part is down because different asset classes (stocks, bonds, cash, and so on) seldom move in the same direction.

dividends   Portions of a company's profits paid to its owners, the stockholders. Not all companies pay dividends; the board of directors makes that decision. Companies that don't pay dividends reinvest the profits in the company to finance additional growth. Financial professionals refer to these companies as "growth" stocks and companies that pay regular dividends as income stocks.

dollar cost averaging   An investing technique that makes regular deposits of the same size in an investment account, regardless of market conditions.

Dow Jones Industrial Average   Also known as the Dow, this index is the best known and most widely quoted in the popular press. The Dow consists of 30 companies that are considered leaders in their industries. Together, they account for a significant amount of the value in the market. Although it is not as reflective of the whole market as other indexes, the Dow is watched earnestly.

economic indicators   Key measurements of the economy's health—unemployment, wages, prices, and so on—gauging the health of the economy.

economic risk   The danger that the economy could turn against your investment. An example is a real estate company in a period of high interest rates.

fixed annuity   Offers a guaranteed interest rate during the accumulation phase and a variety of guaranteed payout options.

growth stock   A stock that usually pays no dividends but puts profits back into the company to finance new growth. Investors buy growth stock for its potential price appreciation as the company grows.

income stock   Pays out current income in the form of dividends. Utilities are good examples of income stocks because of the strong dividends they pay.

index   A way to measure financial activity. An index has an arbitrary beginning value; as the underlying issues change, the index either rises or falls.

large-cap stock   Any company with a market capitalization of $7 billion or more.

liquidity   How quickly you can convert a financial instrument into cash. A mutual fund/subaccount is liquid, while an apartment building is not very liquid.

loaded fund   One that charges a sales fee or commission to the buyer. The fund pays the fee to the broker who sold the shares. The load may be up front or deferred.

management fee   The mutual fund company charges the management fee, also called the investment advisory fee, to pay the fund's manager, who is responsible for making sure that the fund/subaccount meets its objectives.

market capitalization   A way of measuring the size of a company. You calculate it by multiplying the current stock price by the number of outstanding shares. A stock trading at $55 with 100 million outstanding shares would have a market cap of $5.5 billion.

market cycles   Periods of up markets and down markets.

market indicators   A collective name for a number of indexes and other measurements of market activity.

market timing   The attempt to know when market lows and highs are going to occur. This almost always fails over the long run.

market value risk   The danger that your investment will fall out of favor with the market.

midcap stock   Any company with a market capitalization of $1 to $7 billion.

mutual funds   These represent a pool of individuals who have pooled their money and hired a professional management company to invest their money. Each mutual fund has specific goals and objectives that drive its buying and selling decisions. Mutual funds may invest in stocks, bonds, or both.

NASDAQ The NASDAQ, also known as the over-the-counter market, is the new kid on the block. NASDAQ executes trades electronically over a network of brokers. Many of the companies listed here are fairly young, and this is the home of many of today's high tech stars.

Nasdaq Composite Index Covers the NASDAQ market of more than 5,000 stocks.

National Association of Securities Dealers (NASD) A self-regulatory body of securities brokers. The NASD licenses and examines brokers and handles consumer complaints.

net asset value The mutual fund equivalent of a share price. This is the price you pay when you buy into a mutual fund. Unlike stocks, mutual funds have no problem with fractional shares. However much you deposit gets divided by the NAV to arrive at your shares. The mutual fund calculates the NAV by subtracting the liabilities from the holdings of the fund and then dividing by the outstanding shares.

New York Stock Exchange (NYSE) The oldest and most prestigious of all stock exchanges. The NYSE is home to most of the "blue-chip" companies.

New York Stock Exchange Index This index covers all the stocks on the NYSE, making it a broad measurement of larger companies.

no-load fund One that charges no sales fees or commissions up front or deferred.

payout phase   During the payout phase of an annuity, the life insurance company guarantees a specific schedule of payments.

portfolio   The collection of all your investing assets.

preferred stock   As the name implies, preferred stock is a different class of stock with additional rights not granted to common stock owners. Among these rights is first call on dividends.

premium   An insurance company word for contribution or payment into the annuity.

probate   This is the process by which an administrator or executor manages and distributes the property according to the terms of a deceased person's will.

prospectus   A legal document that potential shareholders of mutual funds/subaccounts and initial public offerings of stocks must have before they can invest. It lists complete financial details of the fund as well as the associated risks.

qualified retirement plans   The Internal Revenue Service authorizes qualified retirement plans, and they must adhere to certain rules and regulations. Participants in the plans, often sponsored by an employer, may accumulate money in their accounts on a tax-deferred basis.

return   Another way to say "yield"—and you express it most often as a percentage.

risk Measures the possibility that an investment will not earn the anticipated return.

risk tolerance A way to judge how much risk you are willing to take to achieve an investment goal. The higher your risk tolerance is, the more risk you are willing to take.

Roth IRA The Roth IRA differs from a regular IRA in several ways, chief among them the fact that contributions are not tax-deductible, but withdrawals are tax-free. There are income restrictions and withdrawal schedules.

Russell 2000 Index The Frank Russell Company, now a part of Northwestern Mutual, developed this index of 2,000 smaller companies. It also has numerous other indexes that measure other market segments.

S&P 500 An index developed by Standard and Poor's that measures the health of the market's larger companies. Because it is a broad measure (500 companies), many consider it more reflective of the market's condition than the Dow. It is the benchmark used by most financial professionals to represent "the market."

Securities Investor Protection Corporation A private government-sponsored agency that provides insurance to protect your assets at a brokerage firm if the brokerage fails. Coverage is up to $500,000 per account. The insurance does not protect against trading losses.

SEP IRA   A retirement plan for self-employed people or owners of small businesses that allows them to contribute directly to employees' IRAs.

small-cap stock   Any company with a market capitalization of $1 billion or less.

subaccounts   Another phrase for mutual funds. They reside in the separate account of a variable annuity. The money manager frequently clones an existing mutual fund into a subaccount for the variable annuity.

surrender value   What the account is worth at any point in time. That may be the invested premium plus interest, minus fees and withdrawals. If you withdraw early, there would be penalties and surrender charges deducted.

tax-deferred   This refers to investment vehicles that allow principal and interest to grow without paying taxes on the earnings until sometime in the future. Qualified retirement accounts allow tax-deferred growth. Annuities, whether qualified or not, also allow tax-deferred growth.

tax-free mutual funds   These invest in bonds that provide tax-free income.

transaction fees   Can be fees that charge for just about any service provided by a financial institution, including mutual funds/subaccounts.

turnover   In the mutual fund industry, refers to what percentage of a fund's holdings are bought and sold each year. The higher the turnover is, the higher the expense ratio and tax liabilities will be.

value stock   A stock that the market has under-priced for whatever reason. Often a stock's only sin is not being a part of the current hot sector.

yield   Another way to say "return"; financial experts express it as a percentage. For example, yield is the percent returned to stockholders in the form of dividends.

Web Resources

www.variableannuityonline.com
Annuity.com offers information on immediate and
fixed annuities, CD-type annuities, equity-index
annuities, and quotes, with rates updated daily.

www.annuities-central.com
Annuities-Central.com has several helpful articles
and resources on fixed and equity-indexed annuities.

www.annuitybid.com/edcenter/buyerguide
AnnuityBid.com is one of several sites listed
here that provide information about annuities
in addition to quotes.

www.annuiweb.com/news/news_main.asp
AnnuiWeb is a useful resource with a series of articles that branch from one topic to the next, starting at a beginner level and moving to more
advanced topics.

www.annuityadvantage.com/equityindexed.htm
AnnuityAdvantage.com has a good article on
equity-indexed annuities, along with information
on other types of annuities.

www.fool.com/retirement/annuities/annuities. htm

Fool.com is an irreverent site of information and advice. These writers are not big fans of annuities (or anything else except their own advice, for that matter), but they have some excellent points.

www.immediateannuities.com

ImmediateAnnuities.com is one of the most helpful sites on the web. Its handy free calculator can give you an idea of what a fixed annuity might pay. You don't have to register or give any personal information. The site gives you a quote and shows you optional payout. It also gives you the opportunity to contact someone about buying an annuity, but there is no obligation.

www.nasd.com/Investor/Alerts/ indexed_annuities.htm

This article from the National Association of Securities Dealers (NASD) alerts investors to some of the concerns about equity-indexed annuities—important reading if you're considering this type of annuity.

www.sec.gov/investor/pubs/varannty.htm

This section on the SEC website deals with variable annuities and is worth a look.

Index

H

I

G

J–K

L

Q

W-X-Y-Z